The Rent-to-Rent Blueprint

Making Money from Rental Property

Napa Bafikele

First published in 2018 by Napa Bafikele

ISBN: 978-1079479-61-4

"Ye are the light of the world. A city that is set on a hill cannot be hid" (KJV)

Matthew 5:14

Dedication

I would like to dedicate this book to my daughter – Eden - destiny, my inspiration, motivation and the one who changed my outlook on life.

Napa Bafikele

The Rent-to-Rent Blueprint

Making Money from Rental Property

Contents

Acknowledgements

I would like to thank Ashley Banfield, my mentor, for being the first person who taught me about Rent-to-Rent. Ashley was kind enough to help me with my personal battles and was always there.

I would like to thank every single person who believed in me, by doing a joint venture with me as well as helping me along in my journey.

I would like to thank Kwame MA McPherson and Vinette Hoffman-Jackson for helping me write, edit and publish this book. Their knowledge and skills have been such a massive help.

I would like to thank my mum, Bay Nsakala, for her love, support and encouragement, kind words and warm heart all of which were hugely appreciated. I would like to pass my gratitude to my dad, brother and sister.

Finally, I would like to thank and pass on my gratitude to my family, friends and acquaintances who played their part in my Rent-to-Rent journey, the list was far too long to put everyone here but I would like to say a special thank you to all.

Foreword

When I first met Napa back in 2014, he was a hungry young man looking for his own success and chose to do this via property. What stood out for me with Napa was his genuine hunger to learn and execute as quickly as possible.

Following the one-day Rent-to-Rent course and subsequent mentoring, Napa quickly executed, with conviction and a true desire to stand out from the crowd. As you read this book you will get to know him as I do and realise he was super genuine and was always focused on the end game – success. His ability to teach others has helped them to succeed as he has.

When Napa asked me to write this forward, I questioned him (interrogated him) about why he thinks he can teach others and why I should put my name out there as part of this book. His answer was simple. He sent me his list of properties, his income and stated that I should remember when he started with me, he was made redundant from his job and then homeless. Yes, you read correctly – No job and no home. As I remember those moments, I recalled why I chose to work with Napa in the first place - he will never give up on himself or others and always finds a way to make it happen.

This book was an outline of what Napa did to get over those hurdles and how he has continued to be super resourceful with all that challenges him. You too will learn about the character you perhaps need to succeed in this dog-eat-dog world today. This book will teach you about being true to yourself as you learn from somebody who was just that, himself, rare currently. The industry of property and property training needs more entrepreneurs like Napa, it will show those new to this world that genuine was best. You will learn from the experience of real-life deals, real people and real business systems for Rent-to-Rent. Zero rubbish, zero hype, just Rent-to-Rent business.

Although a quiet person by nature and almost reserved, Napa has catapulted himself as a figurehead and go to person for Rent-to-Rent simply by his actions. As you read you will learn how Napa can transform your property cashflow and lead you into financial freedom that you crave along with a life of choices and freedom. Enjoy.

Ashley Banfield
Property Developer, Trainer and Mentor

Napa Bafikele's book, *The Rent-to-Rent Blueprint*, is a real eye opener. This amazing book provides you with all the information you need, so that you can start making money from renting properties you do not even own. No, I am not talking about anything illegal here, this is 100% legitimate and better than that, it works.

His story is an amazing one; one of those true "rags to riches" tales we all like to hear. Born in the Democratic Republic of the Congo, his family moved to the United Kingdom when he was only a small boy. This migration caused his life to be filled with struggles, from the difficulty of going to school and his inability to speak the English language to starting his own business; without any venture capital to speak of. But he overcame all of that and is now a successful businessman. Napa makes no claims to be the best around or to having the biggest business but he recognises his own success and is grateful at how it came about. Better yet, he knows how to pass that success along to others.

The system that Napa uses for Rent-to-Rent, is one that will work anywhere where housing and money is tight and that is just about anywhere in today's market. In other words, it is something you or I could do, just as easily as he has. No, this is not a get rich scheme. It is a plan to make a growing, successful business but better than that, it is a plan which anyone can do, if they are willing to put in the effort. The information that Napa provides is enough to prove how effective this business model can be as well as give you the basic outline of how to get started. And really, you can be making money quickly, with the potential for rapid growth.

If you are looking for a new direction for your life - a business you can do, a way to make the money you need - then I would say that this book is for you. More than that, this book will encourage you as Napa's overcoming the odds story is something, we all need to do at one time or another, if we are going to be a success. His story and his experience are the proof that you too can do it since all it takes is getting tired of where you are right now and hungry enough for something better...

I highly recommend *The Rent-to-Rent Blueprint*. This could be the plan you have been looking for. Give it a try, see if you can get out of the financial box you are in and become the success you always wanted to be.

Chis'mere Mallard
Entrepreneur and International Speaker

About the Author – Napa Bafikele

Imagine...

Standing in the middle of Sainsbury, hungry and staring at sandwiches, trying to decide which one to purchase. It is your first meal of the day and you have no idea what tomorrow would bring, but in this moment, you are still grateful for life and the fact that you could buy food. You make your selection and head to the cashier to pay. The lady behind the till takes the sandwich, scans it and said to you, "That'll be £3.40 please!" You take your debit card from your wallet and insert it into the machine. It beeps then one word flashes on the display screen - *Declined*. You glanced around embarrassed, clear your throat although there is nothing there, then politely and quietly you ask the lady to try again. Once again, the word flashes across the screen - *Declined*. You swiftly take your card, give no explanation, offer no apology and avoiding any eye contact with the cashier, briskly walk to the nearest cash machine. You insert your card and select Balance. The figure displays - *£0.89p Available*. There is not enough to buy a simple sandwich to quell the hunger pangs as your stomach growls. This was me three years ago, but how did I get here?

My Story

In 1992, I was born in the Democratic Republic of Congo, spending my first ten years, relatively carefree and happy. One of my fondest childhood memories was boasting to my cousin that someday I would be rich, even though I had no idea when, where or how. We would exchange stories of grandeur and each time the story was told we would embellish it even more. Looking back, I suppose it was every child's dream but only a few people pursued beyond that childhood dream.

When I was ten years old, I migrated with my parents and older brother, to live in the United Kingdom. I remember the excitement from my other family members on the morning we headed to the airport, everyone wishing us well. My favourite cousin with whom I had exchanged my daydreams was there too and we hugged, said goodbye and promised we would see each other when we had made our dreams come true. I felt as if going to England would mean a better life for us and my chance to fulfil my dreams and during the long flight, I imagined my bedroom full of lovely furniture and all types of gadgets. My dream of becoming rich had started and I was excited.

When I arrived in the United Kingdom, it was nothing like I had imagined, and things did not go as I had envisioned. I could not understand anyone and that was the biggest shock. Everyone spoke in English when I only spoke Lingala (the Congolese language) and I was immediately scared but I had not shown it especially to my Dad who I felt would never understand. My Dad was impatient, intolerant and not the hugging type of father I yearned for and even at that young age, I learned that he would never change so I never bothered trying. My mother on the other hand, was always smiling and cuddling my brother and I, making up whatever emotional comfort we failed to receive from our Dad.

The second shock came when we arrived 'home'. Home was a studio flat in Highbury, Islington. I remember opening the closet doors, expecting them to lead into bigger rooms, but it was just one room. It was not even a big room, just an ordinary English lounge. Coming from Africa where we had acres of land to play on, I suddenly felt claustrophobic. We had one double bed and I would sleep on it with my mother and brother while my father slept on the sofa.

Being from a culture that valued privacy, I had not discussed our living situation with anyone and simply accepted it as a change I needed to adapt to.

My first real challenge as a non-English speaking immigrant, in the British educational system was at Shacklewell Primary School, Hackney. I was paired with another Congolese student who spoke English well but knew very little of our language, so communication was very limited. In lessons, I was given colouring pencils and random drawings to fill. I began to feel isolated, but I said nothing since I did not want to disappoint my parents. They were trying their best to make life better and I did not want to appear ungrateful or add any unnecessary stress. And after a few months at Shacklewell Primary School, I slowly started being a bit more sociable as more children started to recognise me on the playground, making attempts to include me in their conversations and games.

One afternoon some boys were playing football and asked me to join. Back home I was always a keen footballer and so I felt comfortable playing and, my skills were much better than theirs. Just as suddenly, all communication barriers were removed as all the boys *spoke* football and I was fluent in that language. Very soon, I became known as *the baller* and the more we played and spoke during break or lunchtime, the more my English vocabulary increased; as it had, so had my confidence.

After I finished primary school, I went on to Islington Green Secondary School and it was there I had my first taste of entrepreneurship. I realised I could buy sweet treats and drinks and sold them at a fraction of the canteen price and still made a profit. I was so focused on my side business that attending class was just a mean to generate new customer bases. Admittedly, I wasted the first few years of secondary school but eventually, in Year 10, I settled down, graduated with ten GCSE subjects. My parents were thrilled, and I felt proud I did not let them down.

After I graduated and between 2008 and 2010, I became a football coach, working for a company in Islington called Access to Sports. I would visit Islington, Hackney and Haringey, delivering football sessions to children in these communities; I really enjoyed this job.

Coming from an African background attending university was a non-negotiable option. My family felt job security was best attained by being educated and securing what they termed 'a good job', and it was unthinkable that success could come any other way. For a moment in my life, I allowed my family to write my story. I have no regret of this period in my life since I believed everything happened for a reason. I learnt many valuable lessons that have contributed to making me the person I am today.

I had always loved sports and I thought I would inevitably follow that route, gaining success in my life. I enrolled at Bedfordshire University to study Sports and Exercise Science. I was an exemplary student, graduating with an upper second class degree. Although I was at university, my entrepreneurial ventures continued. I would help panicked students, who had wasted their time throughout the year, with last minute deadlines or a final exam; by offering tuition, help with their assignments or condensed study materials, for a fee. I was always filled with excitement each time I made some money.

In 2013, I graduated from the University of Bedfordshire and went on to study for a Master's degree in Physical Activity, Nutrition and Health Promotion.

While at university, I applied and got a job working as a fitness instructor at Gold's Gym, this job was easy and relatively enjoyable. After seven months I decided to change my employer in a bid to increase my earnings and moved closer to home. I was still living with my parents and sibling in a now three-bedroom house. I began working at Virgin Active Gym on the weekends and occasionally over time during my university breaks. All was going well but I still felt there was something missing from my life, though I had not known what it was and every day I followed the same routine. But there was no excitement and I started to feel restless.

One morning I left home and arrived at work, as usual. I suddenly stopped at the door to the gym as if I had forgotten something. When it finally dawned on me. I had travelled to work in route mode and could not remember my journey at all. I had settled into a routine and disliked it. Once that realisation hit me, I quickly became bored, yearning for new challenges. The excitement of being a fitness instructor had vanished and I started searching for new opportunities and challenges.

I saw an advertisement for a recruitment consultant and liked the flexibility of the job. It was also a new area and so when I was offered the job, I immediately accepted it. As soon as I started working, I quickly realised that the job was extremely demanding and in order to meet set targets meant working long hours, sometimes without a break. I was working ten days each cycle (ten days of work, three days of rest; seven days of work, two days off and five days of work and one day of rest - repeat) with the added pressure of hitting targets. I had not minded the long hours but felt the pressure and intensity failed to match my salary but I was learning new skills, so I kept giving the job my best. To the targets my supervisor gave me, I was setting my own personal targets just to see if I could exceed them and after a few months I did. This made me fall in love with the idea of controlling how much money I earn each month. However, I quickly calculated that I was only getting a tiny fraction of what I was making for the company, so the idea of having a boss started to wear thin. There were many cases of blatant nepotism too which really irked me, and I needed to escape. I needed to think seriously about my next steps and my future.

A Dream Reborn

I decided to get away from everyone and familiar surroundings just to think on my next move. A silver lining was always in every cloud and my experience as a recruitment consultant really motivated me to take control of my own financial destiny. I booked a two-week holiday to Miami and for the first week, I spent time sightseeing, shopping and treating myself. I deserved the break. Sometimes people forget to treat themselves, even after years of working hard, but it was vital to maintain one's sanity, keeping the mind and body functioning at its optimum. Since I had been a fitness trainer, I always took care of my body and watched my diet, and this trip was to rejuvenate my focus, mental and emotional state and mindset.

After the first week I decided it was time to address the motive behind my vacation - *what were my next steps?* I needed to make a change. It was remarkable how certain things seemed to fall into place once you were in the correct mindset. And as I pondered on my next step, I stumbled across a book entitled: *'Making Money from Property: The Guide to Property Investing and Developing'* by Martin Roberts. This book changed my perspective and I finished reading it in two days and I knew then what my next steps were… It was in property investments.

In the past I had attended several property seminars on HMO's, Rent-to-Rent courses and buying properties at auctions but had no capital to finance my dream, so I failed to take any action. It may have been fate because even though I had no starting capital, I was compelled to continue educating myself in the hope that one day I might venture into property investments. I read somewhere *"that it was better to prepare for an opportunity and not get it than to get an opportunity and not be prepared"*. Investing in yourself is always a positive move and today it is a simple piece of advice I offer to all my clients.

Before I flew back to the United Kingdom, I started researching on the internet, looking for events, books, other success stories and most importantly how to finance my dream. If you do not invest in yourself by taking the right training, you might as well give up on your endeavor since what you get is what you put in. My bank account was feeble, but I knew my passion and desire were enough to push me to find a way forward. Once I had decided on my vision and committed, I became more focused than before and I returned to the UK hungrier and ready. After two weeks the reality hit me - hard. I still had bills to pay so I returned to work, but my heart was not in it. Especially since I had created a mental image of what my life was going to be. Eventually, I was unable to readjust to-working-for-a-boss mindset and constantly thought about returning to Miami where I had enjoyed being in control of my time, reading and dreaming.

Instead, I was faced with a boss shoving targets in front of me.

I was just one step away from quitting when I was headhunted as my CV was uploaded onto REED's recruitment agency website and my details matched their requirements. After contacting me, I was offered an interview, then the job by Joe Wicks - the Lean-in-Fifteen man from *The Body Coach* - and I immediately left my office job.

Though the salary was the same, the biggest advantage for me was being able to work from home which meant I had more flexibility in pursuing my property investment dream. It was not long before I started feeling trapped in my own home and once again the need for personal freedom returned. Once again, I wanted to find an escape route. I felt as if I had a tag and no freedom to leave my own home when I chose to. A week later, The Body Coach fired me because I kept making grammatical errors. I would be lying if I said I was crushed.

Since I still needed a job to pay my bills, I got a job in a call centre and it was the combination of all my previous jobs, magnified. This really affected my self-esteem and I felt my career was going downhill - fast. Instead of getting closer to my dream I was moving backwards, and it seemed further and further away.

I honestly felt like giving up. I thought it could not get any worse, but I was wrong. I came home one afternoon and walked in on a domestic situation. At my age I felt I was a man and so I confronted my Dad about his behavior towards the situation. My Dad felt he was being disrespected in his own home and told me to leave his house. I was fearful about leaving since this was not a part of my plan, especially as I was not financially secure to be independent. Nevertheless, my pride would not allow me to beg and I left home at the age of twenty-three.

I started sleeping in my car as I had nowhere else to go and I was using different gym facilities and friends to get the occasional shower. I was always a spiritual person, but these trials were testing my faith and for the first time in my life, I started to wonder if God was listening. Still, I tried being positive as I still had a car, good friends and a job. It could have been worst, but I decided to stop feeling sorry for myself and started making concrete plans to get out of my situation. This unexpected turn in my life meant I needed to earn more money, so that I could afford to live on my own.

Since I was working part-time, I asked the manager to increase my hours so that I could afford accommodation, food and other necessities. I submitted my request on a Friday afternoon with the expectation of a positive response the following week. On the Monday morning, I rushed into work feeling positive about getting the extra hours and recovering from my temporary setback.

I opened the door, walked into my workplace and froze.

The office was completely empty. The usual buzz and high energy atmosphere were gone. All that remained were a few pairs of panicked eyes and my two eyes quickly joined theirs. I found the manager and even though I knew the answer before he spoke, I needed to ask, 'Did you think about my extra hours?' I mumbled. I sounded emotionless, almost robotic. The manager sensing my despondence, gently asked me to go home and as if to give me a thin line of hope, told me he would call when everything was sorted as there were matters the company was dealing with at that moment. I was numb but told I myself to remain positive despite the circumstances. The next day I sat in a café waiting for my boss to call. The phone rang. I immediately recognised his number and quickly answered. This time he was more direct, I suppose it was easier to deliver the bad news over the phone than face-to-face. He informed me that the company had lost their contract, and everyone had to be made redundant. I was stunned, I just sat there staring into space. I was relying on the job to pay for food, petrol and accommodation. Now I was jobless, homeless and hopeless. I did not know what to do next. I was lost. I wanted to cry but even my tears seemed to have abandoned me. I felt as empty as a shell. There were no emotions, no feelings, nothing. I had not even thought to pray. I was and felt alone. My stomach grumbled and I remembered I had not eaten all morning, so got up and headed over to the nearby Sainsbury to get a sandwich. That was when I got my reality check as my card was declined.

On that Tuesday morning, as I stood staring at the cash machine screen showing a balance of £0.89; I knew right there and then that I never wanted to be in that position again for the rest of my life. I stood at the cash machine listening to my stomach and started to reflect on when I was ten years old in the Congo, happy and carefree. A familiar scene played out in my mind; my favourite cousin and I were sharing our grand plans and all the dreams we had. I closed my eyes, leaned against the cash machine and using the back of my hands to stem the flow of tears. I remembered that my cousin had died from malaria in Congo shortly after I had migrated and in that instant I realised that his dream was over, but I was still alive. My dream was still alive. I decided to make a start on my dream as I had nothing else to lose. Wiping my tears, I walked away from that cash machine a new, focused and determined man. I silently prayed and thanked God that I was still alive as I was going to make my dream come true or die trying. I decided that I needed to be financially independent, to never rely on anyone for *my* source of income.

I researched property mentors and the services they offered. After careful research, going to events and talking to industry insiders, I settled on Ashley Banfield as my mentor. He quoted his price and I told him I would pay. I applied for all the credit cards I could get. I then leveraged all the cash I could borrow from friends and paid my mentor. I was all in at that point as I knew I had to earn to pay my debts. This is the point where many people with dreams would stop because they considered paying for a mentor to be too expensive. However, as the adage goes: *'You don't know what you don't know'*. I wanted to know everything and so needed the skills and expertise from someone who had been through the process and knew all the steps I needed to take. I needed someone who had made the mistakes already so I would not make the same mistakes. I needed someone that could help me fulfil my dream and I knew that I would only get what I paid for. I wanted the best. I decided to enter the property market doing Rent-to-Rent. My mentor helped me with the strategies required to raise finance and was constantly available for any questions I had.

Fast forward three years after my turning point, I am now a successful property investor with a portfolio of thirteen properties. Recent changes in the regulation urged to change some aspects of my business. I am no longer answering to bosses, I now control my own time and most importantly, I am financially independent. I once read somewhere that one of the richest men in the Californian gold rush was the man who sold the spades that the miners needed to dig. If you discover an area where a lot of people are working towards a common goal, find out what they need and supply it to them. I realised early in the game that with Rent-to-Rent and HMO properties, in order to keep the properties looking well managed, most investors employ cleaning companies. Therefore, I opened my own cleaning company to supply the demand. Every business minded individual should work towards creating multiple streams of income, so I am also a trainer and mentor to new and inexperienced property investors.

I am not yet where I want to be and there are still challenges ahead but I am mentally, physically and emotionally ready to face them. At this point in my journey, I would like to help as many people as possible who are seeking to make a change in their life by taking control of their financial future. I am not marketing myself as *the* expert or property guru because I consider myself a student of the game.

I now know the right strategies and obstacles that property investors need and are likely to face. Firstly, I am writing this book to share my knowledge and experience with the hope that people may benefit from using the information to kick-start their dreams in property investments. Secondly, this book would help you to get started on your dream via Rent-to-Rent. So here is my property journey to becoming a multi-millionaire!

Napa Bafikele

Introduction

This book provides details about a property investment strategy popularly known as Rent-to-Rent that I have been doing since 2015. You will find within this book, a step-by-step guide on the processes, legislations and the pitfalls involved in starting a successful Rent-to-Rent business. Using the knowledge and experience I have acquired over the years, I have presented the information in a format that any lay person can easily access. Any technical terms used inside this book are explained in the glossary found at the back of the book. Most people know the traditional way of property investing; purchasing Buy-to-Lets (BTL) or flipping for a profit by adding value or refinancing. However, purchasing a property requires a minimum deposit of 20-25%, solicitor and broker fees, along with other fees that add up to a large amount of start-up capital. One of the biggest incentive Rent-to-Rent offers is the low startup costs. Rent-to-Rent requires minimal financing with the possibility of completing multiple deals simultaneously, thereby creating a massive monthly cash flow over a relatively short period of time.

I was encouraged to write this book by many of my mentees who found the courses I offer gave them valuable information. The main objective is to help anyone who is looking to start a business in the property market. The book provides a low risk strategy that has the potential to create a steady income stream, replacing your salary and eventually enabling you to become financially secure. The Rent-to-Rent Blueprint is written to help you.

What is Rent-to-Rent?

Rent-to-Rent is a simple strategy that allows you to take control of a property that you do not own and derive an income from it. This is achieved by renting or leasing a single-let property using the correct agreement and re-letting each room on an individual basis. The profit margin is calculated by simply subtracting the rent paid to the landlord and other expenses, from the total income of the rooms you have let. As with any business investment, sustainability and longevity is very important. No one wants to invest in a business or industry that may go bust at any time costing them time and money. Rent-to-Rent is one of a few property strategies that involve low startup costs and has the potential to grow exponentially quick.

Why? At present, the United Kingdom is experiencing a rapid population growth due to an increase in migration and the fertility rate. The Office of National Statistics recorded 776,351 number of live births in England and Wales in 2014. A slight decrease than in previous years (.3%) but still a significant number of births for a tiny island such as England. The 2001 census recorded that the UK had a population of 58,789,194 in 2001 which rose to 66,687,031 in 2018, showing a growing rate of .61% per annum. This growth rate means that more people will need somewhere to live, increasing the demand for affordable accommodations. There is no indication that we will experience a decline in population growth within the next ten years. This makes property investment a secure, low risk investment.

Another contributing factor to the population growth is the lowered mortality rate due to improved healthcare and lifestyle changes. People are living longer than before with 18% aged 65 and over and 2.4% aged 85 and over.

Inflation has also helped with the current boom in the market. Property prices are increasing in proportionality to the increasing demand for housing. This makes it harder for people to purchase a home. Recent statistics showed that property prices rose 6.1 times than the average UK earning salary. Homeownership has fallen to its lowest level in 30 years. More people are now opting to stay with their parents until their late 30's, just to save for a deposit.

Based on these facts, fewer people have purchased their first property which results in an increase in demands for affordable rental accommodations.

According to the letting agent Your Move, almost half of UK renters are over 46 years of age. The government have therefore, failed to deliver on the promise they made in 2010, to help more than 300,000 people get a new home. In 2016, less than 50% of the promised houses had been built.

With the current uncertainties surrounding Brexit, it is likely that the housing market may be affected, funneling more people into the rental market.

Population increase, inflation and lack of homes to keep up with demands have resulted in more people living in house-share accommodations, thereby making the Rent-to-Rent strategy a very lucrative one.

Reluctant landlords are now showing significant interest in the Rent-to-Rent strategy because it provides them with longer-term security. Normally an investor rents a property for three to five years. Maintenance of the property is also removed from the remit of the landlord and becomes the investors' responsibility, reducing the extraneous costs usually absorbed by the landlords.

If the property needs any refurbishment it can be negotiated in the initial stages of signing the contract.

Most landlords react favorably to a one-off initial cost as they will not need to invest any more cash for the next three to five years in their property. As most refurbishment costs are usually cosmetic, this issue is not a deal breaker.

If the landlord does not want to invest any money towards refurbishment, then there are various alternatives which can be mutually beneficial to both parties. For example, the investor could complete the refurbishment in lieu of a deposit to the landlord. The costs could also be shared resulting in a win/win for both parties. Landlords also save money annually on fees by working with you, the investor, since there are no agency charges or management fees. Landlords would not need to deal with tenants as they are technically your tenants; so, essentially, the only person the landlord is dealing with is you and your company.

Another benefit for the landlord is property checks during tenancy. The Rent-to-Rent investor will look after the property by conducting regular inspections every 2 months, and in most cases deploying cleaners on a weekly or fortnightly basis.

"Own nothing but control everything"

The Rent-to-Rent model is about control. Whilst you did not own the asset, you could still earn from it. There is a famous quote by Nelson Rockefeller that states *"The secret to success is to own nothing, but control everything"*. A strategy that has been successfully implemented globally by well-known companies. Uber's net worth is approximately US$5.9 billion but how many cars does Uber own? The answer would be none. Uber owns no cars but control cars globally; making them a billion-dollar company. Air BnB is another multibillion-dollar company that operates globally. How many properties do they own? None.

You do not have to purchase or own physical assets in the traditional sense to make money from it. The invention of the World Wide Web has made the impossible possible. The same premise exists with the Rent-to-Rent strategy. Property investors do not own the property, they simply control it and make money from it.

Chapter 1 – Mindset

Setting the Mindset

The start of any new venture in life begins with having the right mind-set. This is vital for success. Most unsuccessful people usually share one common trait; they are often very closed minded when it comes to new ideas, taking risks or stepping out of their comfort zone. They prefer the security of the known and even when the current situation is not working, they opt to remain there. Einstein once said, *"The definition of insanity is doing the same thing repeatedly but expecting different results".* This describes a significant percentage of the population. We moan and complain about our jobs, our lives and the lack of cash. However, few are willing to change their routine in order to see the changes in their lifestyle and reap the success they desire.

A closed mindset limits your ability to see the longevity in any new venture you may be thinking about. Inside your mind there is always a struggle, where walls and barriers to success are constantly being erected until they eventually railroad any dreams or aspirations you may have had. People who are closed minded tend to be very negative, constantly creating excuses as to why they have no set goals or why they have not yet achieved any goals. To be a successful entrepreneur, it is imperative that you create a positive and open mindset. A mindset where you believe anything is achievable with the right execution. Your mindset will determine how far you go in this business. Your mindset will help you persevere when challenges arise because it will keep you focused on the end goal and hold you accountable to your greatest critic; You!

Identifying Your WHY

If you have ever attended a property course, you would have constantly heard the phrase: Do you know your WHY? Have you found your WHY? or what is your WHY? Having a why is important. According to Dr. Alex Lickerman, an American psychologist, knowing the reasons (why) for things helps shape how we respond to them. Imagine if someone randomly comes up to you and instructs you to sit in a corner by yourself when everyone else is standing. What is the first question you would ask? Yes, you've guessed it, why? Why is also one of the first lines of enquiry toddlers use in order to understand the world around them? If you are a parent, you can identify with the thousands of times a small child will ask why? Our why is the driving factor behind any success, whether you acknowledge it or not. Having your WHY will equip you with the resilience you need to overcome any obstacle that may have stopped you from moving forward, especially when business becomes difficult.

My WHY, at the time I started my property journey was, I simply did not want to remain homeless. I needed to earn money in order pay my rent. Having a WHY is like laying tracks for an oncoming train. I had to keep moving or get run over. This was a goal I had to constantly work on. Having no goals can make you lazy or give up quickly due to the lack of immediate positive results. Many books will talk about goals, but few will tell you that your goals need to grow and change as you get closer. Most people set static goals such as buying a house but when they achieve these goals, the inevitable happens. Their momentum slows and they pause because they have achieved their preset goals. At this point you can make very foolish decisions that can set your progress back years.

This happened to me when I finally achieved my goal and secured my own accommodation. I began making money through properties. I hired a property manager and took time off to travel the world. I made numerous frivolous purchases that did not grow in value and slowly became liabilities, draining my cash reserves. I purchase two high end two vehicles - a Jaguar XF and a Mercedes Benz. I would take the girl I was dating at the time on shopping sprees and tell her to purchase anything she wanted, at my expense. Since I had achieved my monetary goals and had nothing to motivate me to achieve more, I senselessly spent money. Set short term, medium term and long-term goals, revisit and revise these as you achieve little milestones. Once your short-term goals are achieved, then your medium-term goals need to become your short-term goals. This now means you need new long-term goals. This should be your goal cycle. Napa's revolving goals cycle is included in my course. In terms of finding your WHY and having the motivation to start any business, you first need to take a deep introspective analysis before you start your journey. Know your strength and weaknesses and take time to discover your why.

Don't forget to celebrate each milestone you achieve. It helps to develop your positive mindset and it will drive you towards greater successes. Remember life only ends when you die, life keeps moving and you have got to move with it, or life will leave you behind. To help find your why, try to attend some property training organised by experienced property investors with proven track records. This will not only give you an instant buzz but will provide invaluable insider information on the reality of this business. Being informed may help to not make some avoidable mistakes.

This business is a people business and people do business with people they like. People can usually determine if they like you within the first thirty seconds. If you are to survive in this business long term, you need to create a likeable persona that elicits trusts. You must always present an amicable façade. Regardless of how nicely you may have decorated your rooms, if the person doing the viewing did not connect with you, the chances of them renting from you is significantly reduced.

Invest in yourself to create the person you want to become. Knowing who you are will allow you to work on the required skills and characteristics that are needed to make you successful in this business. If you identify this as a major weakness and you need time to develop the requisite skills such as talking to people and engaging socially, I advise you to find a business partner who has these skills and form a complementary liaison that works for both parties. This will give you time to develop your skills until you are confident to do the business independently.

The next logical step in the process of becoming a property investor is knowing where you are going. If you have no idea where you were going or where this business is taking you, then it might be a challenge for you to succeed. Once you decide that Rent-to-Rent is the property strategy you want to pursue, carry out your research, determine how much money you need to become financially independent, after this you need to figure out your next steps. Remember I told you that you need moving goals to keep yourself motivated to gain more success. Possible questions you could ask yourself are: Should I use my portfolio to scale up? or, Should I use Rent-to-Rent as a vehicle to get me out of the rat race? These are just a couple of questions you needed to ask yourself before commencing any property strategy.

Next, find your exit strategy. According to Investopedia, a□business exit strategy□is an entrepreneur's strategic plan to sell his or her ownership in a company to investors or another company. An exit strategy gives a business owner a way to reduce or liquidate his stake in a business and, if the business is successful, make a substantial profit. For Rent-to-Rent investors, some possible exit strategies include selling your portfolio or returning the properties to the owners once you have achieved your goal. The exit strategy can also come during the tenure of the business before you have achieved financial independence. For a practical example, let us say that you took a property that worked out on paper, meaning the figures showed a clear margin of profitability, but you struggled to make it work. The exit strategy could be a clause written in your contract making it possible to serve notice to the landlord within a reduced time period, or provides you with the alternative option of renting the property as a single let to break even. Be mindful that your exit plan could also be impacted on by new or changed legislations within the industry. It is a common mistake made by long term investors and one that is not often discussed by most business mentors.

Lastly, identify a specific time period for your Rent-to-Rent investment. This will help you to focus and provide some pace in getting to your goals. When I started my Rent-to-Rent business, I wanted to stay in the game for a maximum period of three years. I had a clear exit strategy in place. After three years, I planned to cross over into the buy to let and purchase-lease options then build up my portfolio. Because I had a very clear plan in place, I structured my business plan accordingly. The reason behind this strategy was the benefits derived from an income and capital growth perspective. The Rent-to-Rent strategy does not have the luxury of facilitating capital growth or owning the asset. My exit strategy should not deter you from investing long term in the Rent-to-Rent market. You can do it for as long as you choose. I am merely sharing my exit strategy plans.

Finding Your Financial Freedom Figure

I have mentioned the term financial independence repeatedly, but what does it mean? How much money is required to realistically determine one's financial freedom? Obtaining a financial freedom figure is very important. Most people have the preconceived idea that this needs to be a large figure. In reality it can be quite a low figure. If you live a very modest life, then your financial freedom figure could be very low relative to another person from a different background. Some people may become financially independent from just one property deal. To find your financial freedom figure, analyse your current lifestyle and factor in all necessities. Necessities are the things that are vital for your basic survival, such as rent, food and clothing. At this point you may even discover a few areas in your life where money is being wasted. Detailed analysis of bank statements usually reveals payments that you may have forgotten or no longer need. My advice is to cancel any standing orders you no longer use. In my initial sessions with my mentees, we examine these figures rigorously. Once you arrive at a specific number, that becomes your target figure. You would be surprised how empowering it can be just to write this number down on a piece of paper. It gives you something to aim for and every decision somehow becomes aligned to the achievement of this figure. It is perfectly reasonable if you want to change this figure during the process. There are no guarantee absolutes in life.

Case Study – 1

After securing my first deal with a joint venture partner, he was kind enough to allow me to move into the property. This meant that the property would not be able to maximise cashflow as I was living there - rent free. To build a relationship with the agent, I gifted him a bottle of Moet Champagne. Two weeks after securing that deal, I was at the gym training when I suddenly received a phone call from the agent, telling me to stop whatever I was doing and meet him at a property. I stopped half-way through my workout, did not even take a shower, jumped in my car and drove straight to the address he texted me. When I arrived, we entered the property - a four-bedroom house with a separate large reception room. My property mind was already engaged, and I already started converting the separate reception room into a double room. There was also a good size kitchen with a decent size conservatory.

Using my laptop's deal analyser I quickly calculated the numbers then using www.spareroom.com, I calculated the supply and demand within the area. The property was in a different location to my first but was only twenty minutes away. It was a reasonable commute for me. This agent totally understood my model and as I calculated the numbers, he said, "I told you it would work." We both laughed. I then contacted my joint venture partner and emailed him the due diligence profile I had done. He responded immediately and was very happy with the numbers. Right there, I made an offer and it was accepted. Since they already had my details, the referencing took little time and we collected the keys for the property shortly after. This property was not even on the market. When the agent contacted me, he had collected the keys from the landlord. A couple of hours later, he also found a tenant which made both parties happy. These are the benefits that come with crafting positive working relationships early in your journey. Below are the initial payments made to secure the deal; the original market price for the rent was £2,000 and we offered £1,800 for a 3 years' period.

Type	£
Rent:	1,800
Deposit:	2,492
Admin fee:	498
Reference fee:	37
Move in Fee:	120
Furniture/Decoration:	1,200
Total:	**6,147**

Monthly Cost:	£	Income:	£
Rent:	1,800	Room 1:	650
Council Tax:	150	Room 2:	650
Water:	30	Room 3:	620
Broadband:	29	Room 4:	600
Gas/Electricity:	171	Room 5:	450
Cleaner:	40		
Total	**2,220**	**Total:**	**2,970**
Profit:			**750**

Chapter 2 – Rent-to-Rent Pitfalls
My Personal Experiences

Even though Rent-to-Rent is a great strategy that you can use to create massive cashflow, there is a darker side to it. The side I believe those in the property world seldom talk about. From my experience, if you go onto the various social media platforms such as Facebook or Instagram, you will witness people boasting about the massive amount of money they are making from Rent-to-Rent. They very rarely speak about the challenges that they face. I firmly believe that if you are going to teach people the strategy, it is better to highlight the challenging aspects of that strategy instead of selling false dreams. I consistently receive a high number of private messages, from people asking for help when they run into unforeseen difficulties. They bought the dream but did not factor in the possible pitfalls. I find this unethical and it contradicts my moral viewpoint. People should be made aware of the reality of property investments instead of being sold a fairytale.

For any business to be successful you must invest time, effort and money before you start reaping the rewards. Things will go wrong despite giving it your best. It is called life, so prepare for it.

I have decided to share some of my own challenging experiences. Other people have been kind enough to offer their stories too.

Losing £12,000 in 4 months

I lost approximately £12,000 in 4 months from one property. This property was in a very good location, less than a 15-minute walk to the town centre, with lots of nearby amenities, adequate transport links and recently refurbished. I had similar property types in the area and according to my calculation I should have been making about £800 profit per month. However, inexplicably we struggled to rent the rooms. The rooms in our other properties located in the same area, were quickly rented by prospective tenants. There was no feasible explanation.

I told my property manager to reduce the room rental prices which he did. Still no success. We started advertising on multiple platforms to increase the odds or finding tenants, but still no luck; it was still not moving while simultaneously advertising on other platforms. After a few nerve-wracking weeks, we finally had someone request a short stay from Air BnB and we gladly accepted.

One of the cheapest rooms was also taken by one person who came to view. We conducted all the necessary background checks and this individual passed everything on paper. However, this guy turned into a different person once he moved in. He started abusing the tenant we got from Airbnb about his sexuality and calling him names.

We had to intervene and try to resolve the escalating conflict. He was told that he could not behave in that manner. The behavior and responsibilities of tenants were clearly outlined in the Moving-In booklet pack which is given to every tenant in my portfolio. He was informed that if he could not conform then he would be served a notice to vacate the property. This individual however, knew the law and manipulated it to his advantage.

He told us that if we wanted to evict him, it would take two months for the notice to be served and in that time, he would refuse to pay any rent. His reign of terror did not stop there as he was determined to disrupt the normal running of the property. Each time we brought people in for viewing he would begin to make it unpleasant for us. He would inform the prospective tenants that we had not communicated with him about conducting viewings. To further placate this individual, we transferred the Airbnb gentleman to another property so that he would not be abused and encouraged him to report the matter to the police.

We thought the situation could not get any worse as we tried to wait on the legally required time to elapse. We were horrified when he upped his antics and invited his friends to move into one of the rooms.

Bear in mind that we were still responsible for this property and all the associated costs had to be absorbed. With no income coming in, the expenses quickly added up. After numerous discussions we eventually came to an agreement on how to evict him legally, but the damage had already been done - financially.

It is important to be calm in these situations and try not to add fuel to an already volatile situation. Even though we were exasperated, we maintained our cool. This falls under risk assessment. This individual was inside a property that we were paying for and could do substantial damage to the property if provoked. To limit this, we were able to negotiate until he vacated the premises.

The final bill was £12,000.

On another occasion I experienced a lengthy period of voids. Voids are periods where rooms are unoccupied. This significantly affected the business cashflow. I used my experience and knowledge to minimise this, but nothing seemed to work. I am 99%

sure that most people go through the same experience, but they do not share it with others, maybe to maintain the façade they have created. These are just two scenarios for you to consider when starting your business. What is your Plan B?

I had two rooms empty for nearly six months and in the end I to cut my loss and returned the property since it was not bringing me any income. Passive income is making money without actively working for it. When you start your Rent-to-Rent business, it is rare to achieve immediate passive income; unless there are large upfront capital injection or possibly employing people to do the work. In this business, you are predominantly self-employed. This means 9 to 5 is a luxury. Some days may be longer and be aware that tenants may call at any time with emergencies.

When I started, I had to do most of the work, which included sourcing properties, viewing, making offers and building relationships with agents. I also had to manage the administrative side of the business including keeping accurate records.

Once I secured a property, I would do the shopping to dress the property. If you do not own a vehicle you may have to rely on friends or public transport to move from one location to the next. This can be extremely difficult and result in some degree of frustration. If you have a large portfolio, then the magnitude of the task would multiply. Be mindful of this as you begin your property journey.

I would personally select, purchase and arrange all the furniture myself, then paint and decorate each room. I was actively working in the business. I had to be a jack of all trades and master of all.

Once dressing the property was done, I needed to organise and conduct viewings. That required a lot of time flexibility as prospective tenants may request a viewing at odd hours. This means, working on your prospective tenant's schedule. Until you are an established entrepreneur you make the sacrifices. Your time is also required to do administration and spreadsheets to analyse how the business is performing. My business only became fractionally passive after my seventh property when I employed a manager. At the beginning the business I did not earn any passive income, I had to work hard for every cent. Therefore, be wary when you're told about a passive income strategy. Rent-to-Rent does have the potential to become passive but only when you leverage or have systems in place. Do not be too gullible and buy into the hype without research. It is a business which needs to be developed properly as business mistakes are costly.

I spoke with a few friends and asked them to share their reality since they began doing the business, their experiences and what they have learnt so far. This may help to prepare you for when things do go wrong.

Jeremy

A good friend of mine, let's call him Jeremy, had a portfolio of 6 properties and was due to give one back since they had already lost £9,000 from the second year. Jeremy had the property for two years; it was a

7-bedroom HMO that was classified as a grey area between HMO and planning departments. The planning department said the property needed planning to be used as a 7-bed, however, the HMO department stated it was adequate to be used as a 7-bed let. This created a grey area between the two departments within the council. Although the property was in a good condition and looked very nice, it suffered heavy void periods which lost Jeremy £9,000 in one year. The rental amount was overpriced for the area and the property was far from transport links and amenities. In order to fulfil the agreement which was made with the landlord for guaranteed rent, Jeremy had to borrow money from friends and family to keep the business going and this got him into even more debt. Here are the lessons he learnt from this experience:

Jeremy learnt that when taking a property, you should make sure that due diligence is done thoroughly, and a reasonable rental amount is negotiated for the benefit of the business and the landlord;

Jeremy went for the property based solely on aesthetics. He learnt not to go for properties based on appearance but making sure that it was well located, had great transport links and easily accessible to amenities;

Jeremy also learnt to add a one-year break clause and give 2-months leaving notice period in the contract. This will prevent him from losing money and if the property had not worked out, he would exercise the clauses and save money, not getting into further debt to fulfil the agreement.

Curtis

Another friend, Curtis, was making a net profit of £500 per calendar month. Whenever there was a maintenance issue at the property, Curtis would contact the landlord who would take care of the issue. The landlord would interact with tenants and during their conversations he would ask each tenant how much rent they were paying. After having this information, the landlord thought he could do this and make more money for himself. As a result, the landlord served Curtis a notice to hand the property back. This was Curtis's best performing property. He had good tenants and never experienced any void. The landlord took control and informed the tenants he was no longer working with Curtis. He said he oversaw the property and if anyone wanted to stay, they should pay their rent directly to him. There was no clause in the original contract that the landlord could not serve Curtis notice at any time. Although he had violated the contract, it could cost Curtis more money and time to take the landlord to court. He decided not to do so and dropped the case by moving on. Here are the learning points:

Curtis learnt to control and monitor the interaction between his tenants and the landlord. He learnt to be the middleman, instead of letting the landlord manage any property issue, he should manage it and then invoice the landlord;

Curtis learnt to put a communication clause in the contract where the landlord could not contact any of his tenants without his knowledge and approval.

Chantelle

After doing a Rent-to-Rent course, Chantelle sought a Rent-to-Rent deal for eight months but failed to secure one. She had a new company, therefore had no financing and needed to take out a £5,000 loan from an investor. Even though she had the £5,000 to fund the deal, most agencies were turning her away because she had no guarantor. Chantelle got desperate and put herself under pressure by the success stories of other people she saw on social media. Chantelle made a desperate deal with a landlord who had twenty HMO properties. On paper it was a bad deal as the numbers had not stacked up and during her due diligence it showed that double rooms in the area were going for £500 per month but she was charging £600-£650 per month and struggling to fill the rooms. When she took the property, it was in a very poor condition and she spent £2,000 to refurbish it. Since she had no trading record the landlord agreed to sign the contract based on the following: Three years lease and six months break clauses. After the six months, the landlord took the property back, renting it out to students and charging them more. Chantelle ended up losing money as the property was never fully occupied for the six months she had it. The terms of the loan she took did not favor her either and she ended up paying the investor £20,000 in interest. Here were Chantelle's learning points:

Chantelle learnt that it was important to walk away from deals that did not stack up, numerically;

She learnt that when taking out a loan from an investor to ensure that the terms were fair and a win/win for both parties. In the end, she needed to pay a hefty interest as the terms favoured the investor.

Being desperate and emotional led Chantelle into two predicaments: (1) taking a poor deal and (2) agreeing to a poor loan term since she was desperate to take on the deal. This could have been influenced by the success stories on social media where she felt she was failing and needed to get a deal done to feel successful.

In a nutshell never allow your emotions to overpower your intelligence, be very logical when analysing a property deal since at the end of the day it is about the numbers.

Jane

Jane and her friend had done some property flips and owned a few buy-to-lets. Jane's friend went to work with someone else and quickly realised that this was not for her, channeling her to do more property courses. She came across the Rent-to-Rent strategy and contacted a course leader expressing her eagerness and hunger to be successful. She wanted to leave her job and the course leader told her she would need a good cashflow to leave her job and that Rent-to-Rent was the fastest strategy to do that. Jane wanted to leave work because she was unhappy with the constant organisational changes – she has already had six managers in two years. In addition to this, the relationship with her current manager was frayed.

According to the course teacher, Jane had it all on paper since she had money to start her business and could also act as a guarantor whenever required. Jane needed £5,000 to be financially free and to focus on her Rent-to-Rent business. She started contacting agents and kept getting numerous rejections which she failed to handle well. Eventually, she became petrified to call them and this was reflected in the tone of her voice which made matters worse. Within six months she had only managed to secure two property Rent-to-Rent deals. The first deal had a cashflow of £1,100pcm, the upfront cost was enormous, but the room rented very quickly. However, the second property cash flow was £900pcm and the timing of her venture coincided with Article 4 being implemented in the area. It also took a very long time for all rooms to be fully occupied and Jane had to install a Category A alarm which cost £3,000. Jane had maintenance costs that also negatively affected her cashflow. Some of her tenants were rude and disrespectful over minor property repair issues which added more stress. Her learning points:

Jane felt that she could have developed a thick skin to rejection and not give up on calling agents, if she had kept calling agents that would have given her more confidence and built more relationships. However, she was shy of getting more no's, but she now knows that it was just part of the game, accept the no's and move on.

Jane also took on lots of costs in her agreement which affected her. She learnt to give the landlord more of the major costs and her company would only take responsibility for minor maintenance costs.

All these people had their own successes when running their Rent-to-Rent business. However, as you have read, you find that it is just like most businesses. Periods of fluctuations are normal in any business venture.

As I mentioned earlier, I have received many messages from people who are social media gurus crying out for help. Rent-to-Rent is a fantastic property investment strategy but it must be treated like a business or failure will be inevitable. When I speak with people, the most popular question is always, how many properties do you have? This should not be your first question. You should instead ask "what are you generating financially from the properties you have?"

If you have a small portfolio but generating more income, than someone who has a larger portfolio, then you are in a better place. If you are ready to face challenges, invest time and effort to get to your goals then read on. **This is not a get-rich-quick scheme**, it is a business and potentially your dream maker.

Chapter 3 – Winning in Your R2R Business

As I mentioned earlier, everything in life has its ups and downs. When you are a novice you may only know about one side of the strategy, which could be misleading. You may have gotten the information from a friend, a Facebook post or conducted some research. Richard Branson is one of the people I admire in this world for his business acumen. In one of his books, Richard said many people thought he was a risk taker, which may be true. However, every risk he took had been calculated. He explained that his decisions were not random even when they appeared to be. Each decision took time and occurred after due diligence was stringently carried out. After that process he makes his business decision. I decided quite early to adopt the same mind-set when I approached any decision in business.

Despite the pitfalls that come with Rent-to-Rent, if conducted and managed well, it could change your life like it has done mine. This strategy allowed me to find accommodation for myself when I was homeless. It also gave me the cash flow to travel the world and fund my lifestyle. Since 2015, I have not worked for another person because I had no choice. The most important thing for me is that I control the most valuable human resource. Time. Many people sell their time to their boss for a fraction of its actual worth. Until you realise the value of this limited commodity and adopt a lifestyle that empowers you to use it as you like, you will forever be chasing a monthly paycheck as you build the dreams of others.

My specific exit strategies have also allowed me the opportunity to create other business ventures. After discussing the possible pitfalls and challenges, I would like to focus on the positive side of Rent-to-Rent investment and how it could potentially change your life.

John

John found out about Rent-to-Rent in 2015 while working for Tesco in a petrol station. He saw a man driving a nice white Mercedes and asked him what he did for a living. The man gave him his business card. Initially, John was very reluctant to contact the man but after two weeks he mustered the confidence to call him. The guy was happy to meet John for a coffee and John was gob smacked as he did not believe he would agree to meet him.

During the meeting the man told John he was involved in a property strategy called Rent-to-Rent and he briefly explained how it worked. Instantly, John was excited and wanted to be involved immediately, but he thought he needed experience to do it. He took a job at HAART, a letting agency. He was very eager to start, so he started contacting landlords but had the wrong approach. He had not yet registered a company. He wanted to sublet without getting landlord's approval and was very unsuccessful with that approach.

John and I met when he was showing me a property I wanted to view from HAART, and during our interaction he found out that we were in the same age range. I told him I already have five Rent-to-Rent properties in my portfolio. This really inspired him to see that it was possible. We exchanged personal numbers and in early 2016, I taught him the strategy. John had £10,000 saved and with my help he managed to secure two properties the right way this time. He realised that he did not need the experience of working with a letting agency. In September 2016, he quit his job and went part-time with a different company, so that he could have more time with his Rent-to-Rent business. In 2017 John quit his part-time job and went full-time in Rent-to-Rent. He currently has a portfolio of six Rent-to-Rent properties earning a net profit of £4,000pcm. He is financially-independent and is making more money than he ever made working for companies.

John was so grateful for the choice he made when he encountered some family issues and he was able to assume the role of breadwinner without the usual stress. With his cashflow, John was able to take care of his mum. In 2019, John's main focus is to get into single BTL and HMO's. He has his target set and knows his exit strategy.

Daniel

Daniel is a director for South East London Properties and had an Oil and Gas Logistic business in Nigeria. Due to the uncertainty of the industry with pricing being very volatile, he decided to close the business in 2015 and return to the UK. In early 2016, he started a car rental business, renting cars to Uber drivers with a total of six cars. His business in Nigeria was giving him a net cashflow profit of £10,000pm and with that amount of money coming in, he had developed a very expensive and luxurious lifestyle. In the UK, his new car rental business was not registering significant profits, so he decided to work part time for a luxury car company as a chauffeur, picking up celebrities to top up his earnings.

In July 2017, he found out about Rent-to-Rent strategy and started attending property networking events to accumulate more knowledge about the industry and network with likeminded people. Fast forward to November, he registered his property company and came across a deal that required a £7,000 investment to secure. Daniel did not have any money at the time to fund the deal, so he packaged it and sold it to another investor for £1,500. In January 2018, he came across another deal that he was unable to fund, he again packaged it and sold it for £1,500 to another investor.

In February 2018 Daniel took his first deal that required £4,500 to secure. Alongside money he had generated by selling his two previous deals, he was able to fund this deal alone and use his rental company to act as a guarantor. In March, Daniel took a high interest personal loan of £6,000 that assisted him in funding his second deal. While waiting for his return on investment, Daniel contacted a person that he had met at a property event asking them if they knew someone who wanted to purchase a deal. The person said he was interested in Rent-to-Rent but was afraid of the challenges that came with it. The person proposed a joint venture where they both put

50% of the start-up capital and split the profit share 50/50, that deal brought them a net profit of £1,200pcm.

On Facebook, Daniel also managed to build a relationship with an individual who worked with an estate agency. They met a couple times and ended up doing a joint venture to secure the fourth property in Daniel's portfolio. Daniel and his JV partner were able to make their money back within a month after they took the keys for the properties. With the fifth property, Daniel took a loan of £4,000 from a friend, repaying the capital within four months and £800 interest on top. The property brought him a net of £550pcm. The sixth property, in my opinion, was Daniel's most creative way in securing a property with low money down. Daniel saw a property that he liked in his area and since he had already built a relationship with the agent, he gave Daniel the keys to conduct viewings for his tenants. Once the property was fully tenanted, Daniel used that capital to pay for the rent, deposit and administration fee. Simplified, he invested none of his own money to secure the deal - What a genius! This just proves that if you build a great relationship with an agent, it could open many creative ways to secure a deal with low money down.

By January 2019, Daniel was looking to go full time into property investing and required £8,000 cashflow, to consider himself financially free. With his current portfolio, his cashflow net is about £4,000pcm. He believes that within four months, he would be able to fulfil his goal of £8,000pcm.

I first got into Rent-to-Rent because I realised that it could generate a high cashflow without the excessive financial outlay which is associated with the purchase of a property. To be honest, I have found Rent-to-Rent to be a great way to learn about acquiring HMO properties and making them work for you as an investor. HMO investing is not for the faint hearted, especially when done properly - so being able to control a property and benefit from the cashflow is amazing. I was first seriously told about the strategy by a property trainer in the midlands, when the trainer held a Rent-to-Rent Quick Start one-day course, a few years ago. The one-day course explained all that was required to start, and it gave me the insights I needed to act.

Samuel Ikhinmwin

Using Rent-to-Rent has helped me to increase my businesses' monthly cash flow. Additionally, it has allowed me to support people in other aspects of property investment besides the property sourcing activities I was doing before. As the host of the Canary Wharf Property Investors Network meeting, a monthly property networking event, I found that the more rounded I was in my property experience the more value I could give to attendees. The Rent-to-Rent deals we have crafted and used, helped us to get in and out very quickly of deals that could otherwise have taken much longer to secure and monetise for revenue.

Rent-to-Rent enabled me to attain property revenue and allowed me to leave my fulltime employment. The cashflow I have achieved from the portfolio has also acted as another income stream, increasing my monthly cashflow.

Here is another example: Early on in 2018 I negotiated the takeover of an HMO property that was already being operated as a Rent-to-Rent by another managing agent. I happily paid a sourcing fee to the existing operator and took over the property with another business partner. We have since increased the occupancy on the property and invested in a cosmetic refurbishment as well as HMO compliance upgrades. At present the rental guarantee to the landlord was £2,300pcm, whilst the income that we produced on the house with full occupancy was £4,400pcm. Taking into account a monthly expense of roughly £650-£700pcm, this property produced a revenue of £1,400pcm. Considering the deal took roughly three months from the initial talks to handover, I see the Rent-to-Rent approach as a good one to help people who are keen to take productive steps into property. Having participated in deals as lucrative as this, I was inspired to develop the

Sourcing Blueprint, a framework helping anyone who desires to do well in property to focus on the right things in their acquisition efforts. The Sourcing Blueprint can be found here at www.SourcingBlueprint.com.

Jack Wicks

Jack was working at the airport and he hated it. He was looking for other ventures to create a steady income stream. Jack's passion was in property development. So, after a few months looking for alternative employment and with the assistance of joint venture financing, he managed to purchase a block of four flats. He then refinanced and pulled out all the invested money to pay the investor back. The properties had a low cashflow as they were refinanced at a higher rate. Therefore, Jack still needed a regular income, that's when his mentor introduced him to Rent-to-Rent.

Jack completed a Rent-to-Rent course and signed up to a mentorship program with the trainer. It took Jack three months to get his first Rent-to-Rent deal and two and half years later Jack has a portfolio of fourteen Rent-to-Rent properties. The cashflow on his portfolio allowed his brother to quit his job and join him in the business. It also allowed his brother to take control of his time and destiny since he has two children. The flexibility of the new venture means he can now spend more time with his family.

Jack felt that Rent-to-Rent was not just an entry strategy for property investment but a business which provided relevant skills, experience and knowledge to be successful in other property strategies. It allowed him to build a solid relationship with agents, landlords and local tradesmen.

Jack was able to get first refusal with a property purchased on a delayed completion and this was one of his Rent-to-Rent deals. The agreed purchased price was £750,000; the estimation refurbishment cost was £1million with a GDV of £3.4million. The plan was to convert the property into 2 blocks of 6 flats using joint venture finance. Once the project was completed the flats would go on the market for sale.

Case Study 2

Norris was inspired to do Rent-to-Rent based upon the success he witnessed with my journey. Just like me, he did not have any finance to start, however, he was very eager to learn and get started. He joined my mentorship program and immediately I spotted that he had the right mindset and wanted to work with him. You can teach people the techniques and strategies, but they must develop their own attitude and mindset to reap success in any aspect of life.

There are numerous people who want to get involved with the Rent-to-Rent strategy but do not have the time nor the right attitude of resilience. I knew Norris was ready, so I connected him with a friend I had met in the property industry. Under my guidance, Norris went on to secure two Rent-to-Rent deals in London. The joint venture partner provided finance for the deal and acted as a guarantor while Norris sourced and managed the deals.

Monthly Cost:	£	Income:	£
Rent:	2,675	Room 1:	750
Council Tax:	81	Room 2:	750
Cleaner:	40	Room 3:	702
Broadband:	35	Room 4:	702
Water:	40	Room 5:	702
Gas/Electricity	193	Room 6:	624
Total:	**3,064**	**Total:**	**4,230**
Profit:	**1,166**		

Chapter 4 – Company Set-up

We have now covered the pitfalls and the positive side of the Rent-to-Rent strategy. In this section I will focus on the steps I have followed to create a successful Rent-to-Rent business.

Step 1

The first step in starting your Rent-to-Rent business is to create a company. I recommend you consult an accountant on what type of company would be best suited for you since there are different types one could create. I used UKPLC to register a limited company. If you do not want to register a company yourself, you could hire an accountant to do so but be aware that there would be fees, and these will add to your startup costs. There are many other factors that need to be considered before a company formation that cannot be covered here. However, an accountant or your mentor can guide you through the process to ensure you do not make any costly mistakes. Additional information can be found at the following websites.

www.UKPLC.com

www.companyhouse.co.uk

It is important to have a professional brand appearance for your business to distinguish you from novices. Many of your clients will know of you from referrals, business checks or google before they meet you in person. It is therefore extremely important that you are portrayed as a professional to build credibility and establish trust.

There are many ways that you can build your professional brand appearance. Here are a few, but this list is not exhaustive.

Website: Having a website is vital for your business. As you approach agents and landlords, many will ask for your website so that they could browse to get information about you and your company. Having a website is also great for your prospective tenants since they could complete an application form, browse your company or get information about the property they are interested in. If you're looking for a professional web designer, I strongly recommend

Marco you can contact him at info@marcpremierdesign.co.uk.

Business Card: business cards provide a great and professional look when dealing with landlords and agents. My web designer Marco created my business cards or you could use a local printing shop. There are many other websites online, but I recommend that you keep a tight rein on your finances as you are starting your property journey. Business cards do not have to be expensive to give that professional look.

Professional Email: while purchasing a domain for your website you could also add a professional email address, rather than using Gmail, Yahoo or Hotmail. You would have your own company email address, e.g. info@yourcompanyname.co.uk. My personal preference (being UK based) - co.uk – which is more appealing than others, but this is also dependent on the availability of domain names.

Landline: since you are presenting yourself as a company, it would be great to have a landline rather than using mobile numbers. I suggest you use your local landline number. Having a local landline provide your clients with the reassurance and the security that you have a physical base and it helps in building trust and confidence in you. For example, if you are in Bedford it would be great to use 01234 rather than another area code. Visit https://www.ereceptionist.co.uk for more information on how you could set your landline number; even having virtual assistants but this depends on your budget.

Step 2:

The second step is opening a business account with a bank. This once again helps your credibility and is crucial if in the future you would like to seek investors in your business.

The process is usually very straightforward but adverse credit, CCJ's or bankruptcy can have a negative impact on your credit score. Banks may refuse to extend credit, offer you a loan or even refuse to let you open a business account with them. Don't panic! There is always a solution to possible problems that are likely to arise. As finance is one of the areas where most clients struggle, especially if they have checkered financial history, an entire section is dedicated to the various resources and steps you can take to get a business account. See www.napabafikele.com. Prior to starting your Rent-to-Rent business you need finance to fund your deals and this could vary from deal to deal. The start-up capital varies per location and also the structure of the deal. I have not paid above £7,000 for any of my deals. However, capital required per deal ranges from £3,000 to £7,000. This capital is required to finance the following:

First month rent

Deposit

Agency fees

Furniture / Decoration

The Government, from 1st June 2019, will introduce the Tenant Fees Ban which planned to ban letting agents and landlords' fees charged to tenants. Below, examples of banned fees:

Charging for guarantor form

Credit Checks

Cleaning Services

Inventories

References

Professional Cleaning

Having the property de-fleaed as a condition of allowing pets in the property

Admin charges

Requirements to have specific insurance providers

Gardening services

This is a great opportunity for Rent-to-Renters as the entry cost will be reduced, however, company let does not qualify for tenant fee ban. Just be aware that some agencies could charge you for fees and some may not charge you. The agents will find a way to capitalise from the loss which means they could charge landlords more. As Rent-to-Renters do not charge fees to landlord that could make the model more attractive. Another benefit is that agency would like to cut cost and one of the ways is to reduce staffing; therefore, I hypothesize that the service to landlord and tenants would suffer.

When I started, lack of funds was one of the major obstacles I faced until I was shown the different ways, I could raise finance, such as:

Joint Venture or JV

My experience on raising finance through a joint venture I defined as 'two or more parties come together to achieve a common goal'. For a joint venture to work, the parties come together, offering something different from each other to achieve set goals. If they are partners with the same skillsets, the venture may not work since they could get in each other's way. Both partners must have different skills or experiences to bring, for the joint venture to work. So, spending time to know your partner well is important.

A joint venture is like a marriage and the commitment you make among yourselves for the duration of that business could determine the prosperity of your business. Ensure all agreed terms are a win/win for all parties and make sure you discuss anything you are uncertain of or unhappy about. Most importantly, make sure you are transparent. In my first joint venture, my partner provided the finance to secure the deals and acted as a guarantor whenever it was necessary. I sourced the deals and managed them, and we split the profit 50/50. The partner and I were novices in the property industry and went straight into splitting the profit without structuring how he would make his money back.

My second JV partner provided the finance to secure a deal and I managed the property. We split 50/50 on profit. However, this investor was very experienced, and I learnt a lot from him, especially in terms of business and having the correct mindset. He not only provided finance but after engaging with him, I now have the mindset of running my own Rent-to-Rent business. Being new to the business, this was a very handy experience to have and he taught me how to create spreadsheets and keep track of my figures. The investment to secure the property was around £5,000 and it took us five months to make the initial investment back - after the fifth month - we split the profit at 50% each. Therefore, for the first five months of running that particular property I had not made any money until the investor's initial investment was paid.

Having gained more experience in the field, I would not structure any future Rent-to-Rent deal in a similar manner. I would ensure I have 60% of the profit, pay back the capital invested and split the remaining 40% with the investor on a 50/50 share. This is how it would look:

Capital invested: £5,000

Profit: £900

Duration to recuperate investment: £5,000/900 = 5 months

60% of profit: £540 would go onto capital repayment

40% of profit: £360 would be split equally among both parties.

Structuring it this way means you could use the initial finance to fund travel and other activities that are required to manage a property, otherwise you would be using your own finances. This was also a better strategy as it gave you greater control of the money flowing into your business and provide you with liquid cash for emergencies.

There are many ways of structuring a joint venture agreement, however, making sure all parties are happy with the agreement is essential to the sustainability of the business arrangement. Another possible option you could use is to charge a management fee while the investor was making the initial capital investment back and you managed the deal.

Credit Card

You could also use your credit card to fund your deals. You could call your provider to increase your amount and to reduce the interest rate. Many people do not realise that they can pick up the phone and negotiate their credit card terms. In the past when I have use this method, the credit card company simply asked me the reason I wanted to increase the card limit. I always told them it was for holiday purposes or to purchase a vehicle and then use the money to fund any deals. If you mentioned it was for business purposes the likelihood of you being accepted is minimal. I have used this method, not to fund a deal but to pay for my mentorship fees.

Disclaimer: *when you apply this method, it is at your own risk and your responsibility to make any repayments.*

Bank Loan

Another method I used to raise money was a business loan. I had my business bank account with NatWest and managed to raise £5,000 to fund my own deals. Therefore, if you have a plan in place you could approach your own bank, taking a business or personal loan to fund your deals. I recently helped my mentee to get a business loan with Santander by working on his business plan and cashflow forecast.

Do not underestimate the power of a business plan in the process of securing finances. Banks and Joint Venture partners will be happy to help if your plans pass their scrutiny. If you are a fan on the Apprentice, you will notice how stringently this is assessed in determining the success of any business. Don't just download a generic template, get a professional or experienced person to assist you.

Friends / Family

Approaching friends and family is another way. I know many people who have done this. If you have friends who do not have any money, I suggest you implement some changes to your circle. It is said that your network is directly linked to your net worth. I was fortunate that a good friend whom I met at a property event and shared the same mentor, loaned me £6,000 to secure another deal.

Case Study 3

I came across a property that was less than 5-minutes' walk from my first Rent-to-Rent deal. I contacted the agent to arrange a meeting and view the property. I always attend viewings ready to make offers. As I had carried out pre checks for the property I knew the numbers worked well. I then contacted my joint venture partner and expressed my thoughts about the deal. After doing further due diligence we both agreed to put in an offer. As I had put in the offer within 24 hours, the agent got back to inform me that the landlord accepted the offer. We paid the reservation fee and sent details for referencing. Since it was a brand-new agent I had never worked with before.

Strange and unexplained twists sometimes happen in life and the property market is not exempted. Shortly after the referencing process had commenced, I received an email and a phone call from the agent at approximately 6 am the morning after. It was strange because of the time of the call and the urgency in his voice. The agent asked me to pay the first month's rent and deposit. I ignored the message until I was fully awake. When I was fully conscious and lucid, I looked at the email again. It just did not feel right so; I called the agent for more details regarding that email he had sent.

The agent said he was unaware that an email had been sent and his manager promised he would investigate further. During the investigation I received another email later that day asking me to pay quickly otherwise the landlord will pull out of the deal. I immediately contacted the agency again to clarify the emails I was receiving, and he once again reiterated that it was not him.

After a couple of days, the agency got back to me and informed me that their email system was hacked and head office decided not to work with corporate lets anymore. I felt sad as the numbers worked very well and we would have made a large profit from that property.

I was going on holiday that week to Cyprus, but I wanted to tell the manager how disappointed I was that the deal did not go through. He was pro corporate let and wanted to help me but relayed that since the head office had changed the company's policy, he was powerless. He told me however, that the landlord wanted the deal to go through and he was still happy to work with corporate let.

I told the agency manager that I was already booked to go on holiday but if he keeps the deal alive for me, I will reward him with a higher commission fee.

When I was away, the agent once contacted me to let me know the landlord wanted to speak with me as soon as I returned from holiday. An hour after I landed in the UK, I contacted the landlord and arranged to meet at his property, I told him about the property and outlined the benefits for him. I also explained that I owned other businesses which may also need their services. After our discussion, I sent him the contract agreement and he was happy with the terms and we ended up signing the property on a 3-year contract.

Now before we move on, a few people may question the wisdom of going on holiday when a potentially lucrative deal could slip through my fingers. Here I would take the time to explain the difference between acting quickly and acting in haste. You can act quickly but only when you have all the required details and you can make an informed decision. Haste is reactive and you either respond with emotion or without thinking things through.

If I had acted hastily and panicked when the first email came, I would have lost a lot of money. Never react because of desperation or frustration and without all the information.

Monthly Cost:	£	Income:	£
Rent:	2,350	Room 1:	933
Council Tax:	70	Room 2:	750
Gas/Electricity:	170	Room 3:	733
Water:	30	Room 4:	650
Broadband:	39	Room 5:	650
Cleaner:	40		
Total:	**2,699**	**Total:**	**3,716**
Profit:			**1,017**

Case Study 4

This deal was a 'low money down,' and my initial investment was £900. I negotiated with the landlord for a 2 weeks' grace rental period. I also negotiated to pay the deposit in 2 months' time. The property was already decorated and the initial £900 was used to get furniture and kitchen utensils. I collected the first and last months' rent from the tenants which allowed me to pay the rent and deposit to the landlord. As the deal was sourced directly from the landlord, administrative and reference fees were not applicable, reducing the entry cost.

There are so many entry points if you want to get into Rent-to-Rent that the limited availability of funds should never be a deterrent. Using your negotiating skills and a good understanding of the property market means there is always an opportunity available for the right person.

This is the main reason I speak about an open mindset that looks for solutions instead of excuses.

Napa Bafikele

Monthly Cost:	£	Income:	£
Rent:	2,050	Room 1:	900
Council tax:	70	Room 2:	850
Gas/Electricity:	170	Room 3:	700
Water: paid by landlord		Room 4:	650
Broadband:	29		
Cleaner:	40		
Total:	**2,359**	**Total:**	**3,050**
Profit:			**741**

Chapter 5 – Compliance

Step 3

The next step is to get compliant and insurance for your company. Registering to be a member of the National Landlord Association will give you discounts when conducting tenant references. Since you will be operating as a property manager, it is mandatory to join one of three government approved redress schemes which have been in place since 1st October 2014. The purpose of the scheme is to act as a third-party service when a customer has a complaint about your service which could not be resolved amongst yourselves. Therefore, the matter could escalate to the extent where it is sent to the redress scheme. The scheme also ensures that you comply with the legal requirements; this helps to eradicate any opportunity for the property agent/manager to engage in unacceptable practices. These schemes were initiated in order to help regulate and monitor private rented sector standards. The approved three government redress schemes are as follows:

Ombudsman Services Property (www.ombudsman-services.org/property.html)

Property Redress Scheme (www.theprs.co.uk)

The Property Ombudsman (www.tpos.co.uk)

Insurance

Since a member of the public would be visiting your Rent-to-Rent property, you should consider obtaining a public liability insurance. This covers the cost of any claim made if a member of the public was injured on your business premises. If you damaged property belonging to someone else while carrying out business activities this policy covers you. For example, if you carry out a viewing at your Rent-to-Rent property and the prospective client accidently missed a step on the staircase, injuring themselves, your policy would cover the customer's claim for injuries.

Professional Indemnity Insurance covers people in professions where they offer advice, such as solicitors or accountants. The policy will cover you from any claims made against you for your work, advice or negligence.

Employer's Liability Insurance covers employees if they are injured or fall ill because of the work they were doing on your behalf. If you do not have any employees, then this policy may also be deemed irrelevant. However, if you employed someone directly or indirectly to work within your company, then I advise you to get this policy. I took out this policy when I hired a manager to take care of my portfolio.

The Client Money Protection Act will come into force from 1st April 2019. It will protect any money a landlord or tenant pay to a letting agency whilst it remained in the custody or control of the agency. In the event the agency goes into administration or misappropriate a client's funds, it will ensure that the landlord or tenants will be reimbursed accordingly.

Deposit

The Deposit Protection Scheme started on 6th April 2006, for tenants with Assured Short-hold Tenancy

(AST) leases who have paid a deposit. It requires the landlord or agent to protect the deposit by placing it in a recognised scheme. The purpose of the scheme is to ensure tenants received their deposit if they met the terms of the agreement, and did not damage the property and finally, paid their rent and allocated bills. The deposit must be put into the scheme within 30 days of receiving it and the tenant must be informed. Below are the schemes that you could use to protect the deposit:

http://www.depositprotection.com/

http://www.mydeposits.co.uk/

https://www.tenancydepositscheme.com/

Let us say a potential tenant viewed one of your rooms and wanted to hold it by paying a holding deposit. At this point you do not have to protect the holding deposit. However, when the tenants move in, the holding deposit is now protected. If you do not protect the deposit, the court could order you to repay the tenant three times the amount of the deposit.

Therefore, I recommend you protect every deposit you receive.

Registering for ICO

Information Commissioners Office (ICO) was set up for data protection in any business in England collecting or storing data on individuals. Since you would be collecting personal data from tenants and landlords, it is mandatory to be registered with ICO. To register visit www.ICO.org.uk.

HMO requirements

By now your company should be registered and the professional appearance of your company should be in place. The company should be registered to one of the three redress schemes, be a member of the NLA and finally be insured. At this stage it is about researching your area's HMO requirements and whether it is an Article 4 area. HMO stands for House in Multiple Occupation. It is where an entire property is rented out to three or more people, forming two or more households, sharing a communal space like a bathroom or kitchen.

Prior to the 1st October 2018, a property required HMO license if it was occupied by five or more people, forming two or more separate households and comprising three or more stories. For example, my 3rd Rent-to-Rent property was a 3-storey property comprising of five bedrooms. We converted that property into a 6-bedrooms HMO and was granted the license to accommodate ten tenants. The government has now decided to bring mandatory licensing into smaller HMO's and these changes came into force 1st October 2018. The amendment was that any property occupied by five or more people forming two or more households, regardless of the number of stories a HMO license is required. Furthermore, if you had a property operating as an HMO that did not require license after the 1st October 2018, you need to apply for a license through your local council. The new regulation also introduced a minimum room size. Any room that had a usable floor space less than 6.51sqm was prohibited to be let out to a single adult and 10.22sqm for a room occupied by two adults sharing. Furthermore, any room that was under 4.64sqm is not permitted to be used for sleeping and breaches of these conditions could lead to prosecution.

This came into force, imposing a challenge on the Rent-to-Rent strategy, however, this also reduced competition so do not be fearful or allow it to turn you away from finding a solution. After all, it has been said that if one door closes another opens. You could target properties that already had an HMO license since they would not be affected. You could work with the landlord to get a license like I had with my HMO. If the numbers work and there is a good profit margin, you could target 4-bed properties. However, a 4-bed property may not require HMO licensing, but fire regulations would still need to be in place.

Article 4 Direction

Permitted Development Right is when you are authorised to make certain changes at your property without the need of applying for planning permission.

In an Article 4 Direction Area, the permitted development right has been removed. Therefore, if you wanted to change a property's use, you would need to apply for planning permission. For instance, any property that was operating as a single dwelling house (C3), where the landlord wanted to use the property as a small HMO (C4), it needs to get planning permission. The local authority issues Article 4 when they feel the area is saturated with many HMO's and issuing such allows them to gain more control of the environmental impacts of numerous HMO's. However, you could still operate in such areas by targeting properties that already have HMO licenses.

Summary

At this stage you would have now researched your area and got on board with your local authority HMO requirement.

Case Study 5

This deal was recommended to us by a landlord. The landlord for this property had recently spent £80,000 on refurbishment and we were the first people to view the project when it was completed. The property, however, did not have a HMO license. I was very nervous to ask the landlord to apply for the license and fund the required work. Then I remembered the advice my mentor had given me earlier in my journey. My mentor told me to always ask for what you want and don't speculate on the answers before you receive them. Matthew 7:7 it states: "Ask and you will receive. Seek and you will find. Knock and the door will be opened to you". Therefore, when you come across a similar situation do not be afraid to ask, the worst that could happen is the landlord saying no; an answer which will not kill you.

I asked and was surprised when he agreed on funding the license fee and work that needed to be done. I managed the project.

Monthly Cost	£	Income	£
Rent:	2,100	Room1:	850
Council Tax:	151	Room2:	650
Cleaner:	60	Room3:	750
Water:	50	Room4:	550
Broadband:	49	Room5:	690
Gas/Electric:	101	Room6:	450
Total expenses:	**2,511**	**Total Income:**	**3,940**
Profit:			**1,429**

Case Study 6

Beverley enquired about my 1-2-1 Rent-to-Rent property training for her and her husband as she wanted her husband to join the property investment business. Beverley already operates a successful business and had a few buy to lets. The couple wanted to increase their monthly cash flow. Beverley wanted her husband to work full time in property investments and increase their buy to let and HMO portfolio. When I train people, I always like them to identify their why; Beverley and Roland's why was very solid and inspiring. Their main reason for doing Rent-to-Rent was not just to create more financial freedom, they wanted to create enough cash flow for charity work back in Africa.

Roland is a big muscular man and it was clear that he was a man who was secure in the knowledge that the traditional methods of property investments were solid and risk free. During our sessions he would look at me dubiously and shift in his chair as if my forecast and strategies were too good to be true. To be honest, I am quite fit and athletic, but I did squirm a few times during my sessions. Included in my 1-2-1 Rent-to-Rent sessions is a section where I teach you how to speak to letting agents and book a viewing. When I told Beverley and Roland that they would have to call the agent, they became very nervous. As expected, Roland was very skeptical. However, after I coached, coaxed him and gave him my script, he tried and aced it. His success with the agents erased some of his original skepticism and from that point he started to engage more.

After the first introductory sessions, they joined my mentoring program on a gold package. In this package, I work 1-2-1 with clients for 3 months to help them grow their Rent-to-Rent businesses. The remarkable growth I observed in Roland was very uplifting and I felt very excited about his progress. It reminds me of the joy I get when I mentor people. Roland's confidence grew to another level and surpassed my expectations. Less than 2 months after my training, he secured his first Rent-to-Rent deal in London. The property already had a HMO license and had a cashflow of £927.

Chapter 6 – Goldmine Area

Finding demand

Step 4

In step four we will find out about deals and demand. Location is very important, especially when dealing with professional tenants. As a rule of thumb, you want to ensure that the property is near to certain amenities. In London, the closer you are to a tube or train station the more you attract prospects. Also, you need to analyse the demand of your selected area before proceeding. If the demand is low, you would struggle to let the rooms.

There are various ways to analyse the supply and demand in your areas of interest. Recently several, methods have been developed which can help in the process. However, I would recommend speaking to your mentor or someone with experience in the property market as they have the firsthand experience which cannot be replicated on a computer. They will also be quicker to recognise and adapt to change and

121

fluctuations in the market. Another added advantage is of course the human connections which websites do not have. Valuable and crucial information that can make or break deals can be exchanged via a simple phone call that could be missed just checking on the internet.

Finding Deals

In order to find properties, there are two separate avenues which could be adopted:

You could go direct to the landlord which could be the cheapest route as you have more opportunities in negotiating and selling your idea, but it could also be the slowest way to get a deal.

Another way is via a letting or estate agent, this is the quickest route since agents always have stock and sometimes it could be challenging to get them on board as most only worked within a certain criterion. Sourcing a deal via an agent tends to be the most expensive route as well because of upfront cost such as agent fees, first month rent and five weeks' deposit. Some agents even go to the extent of asking for 12 weeks' deposit for a company let. This increases the upfront cost of your deal.

When I started, I was given a script from my mentor and I struggled with being articulate on the phone using that script. It felt unnatural to me and if you were someone like me who struggle with scripts, you would also. Perhaps you could look and amend the script in your own way, keeping the main content. Throughout my years of experience, I have developed my own script which is adaptable to almost any scenarios. The feedback I get from anyone using my script DNA include:

Feedback 1

When I started on my Rent-to-Rent journey, I was so terrified of contacting the estate agents or any landlord regarding properties which I had found. I had no clue on what it is you have to say to get the landlords to hand you their keys. That is until I watched Napa on one of his Facebook lives (TIPS ON NEGOTIATING R2R BENEFITS) and I told myself I must get onto his coaching course and get me this rent 2 rent script (NAPA's DNA script as he calls it).

Once I was on the course, I obtained the script. Not only did Napa give it to me, he also went through it with me to ensure that I understood the content. Napa also did some live calls with me where I fully grasped the practical side of speaking to Estate Agents and Landlords. When Napa was doing this, it looked like second nature to him. I thought to myself it must be easy for him given he is the one that wrote the script, I was in denial that I could do the same. However, when I started calling Estate Agents on my own, following the script I was amazed at how simple it became to speak to Estate Agents.

To perfect my script, Napa instructed me to call Estate Agents that are not in my Gold mine area and record my calls, thereafter he would go through the recordings with me and tell me what I should improve. That made me gain more confidence in the script and what I was saying. Until today, I have not had any negative responses either on the phone or via email. I believe this is because Napa's script touches on building a relationship/ rapport with the Estate Agent and getting the Estate agent interested in what you have to say. Thanks to Napa's script, support and guidance I have managed to secure two Rent-to-Rent properties in my area within two months under his mentoring program (Carol Maisiri Mbaya).

Feedback 2

Napa is an excellent teacher and a master at negotiating. This guy has got serious skills! His knowledge is outstanding and in talks with estate agents/landlords he has all the answers to any questions.

He listens to my future plans and helps me achieve financial freedom. More importantly, he believes in me and gives me the confidence even with my language barriers. I believe he can conquer any task to achieve not only his dreams but also all his mentees. Genuinely, humble, sincere guy it's truly a pleasure to be your mentee. Napa has been mentoring me less than two months and we have secured six Rent-to-Rent HMO's in Manchester (Cristian Crivaci)

My script was developed after consultation with a psychologist and an established speaker to increase the likelihood of receiving a positive response. Negotiation is not just talking or saying words prewritten. It involves other elements that will ensure you are perceived as more confident and helps to instill the right mindset when you need to speak with agents, clients and/or business associates.

The conversation with the agent and or landlord can be quite daunting as you need to convince them within a few minutes that you are capable, reliable and trustworthy. You should also be aware that agents in the same areas may communicate so you need to make sure you get your opening pitch right.

Usually when the agent answers, they tend to say their name and it is good practice to call them by their name to build rapport.

The agent usually asks about your company like how long it has been trading and if it was less than three years, they would likely ask for a guarantor. Be wary as most agencies have a policy of not wanting to work with corporate let companies and others misunderstand how the model works. Do not be disheartened if you keep hearing "no!'

However, you must have a Plan B for those occasions when the response does not go the way you anticipated. Never give up the goal, just change the method.

Property Search

There are many sites that could be used to find properties via agents, however, you could find properties using www.rightmove.co.uk and apply a similar method to other sites.

Enter your location and click to - on to Rent.

The property type you could target are three-bedrooms with one or two separate receptions or 4-bedrooms with 1 reception or more, remember to align yourself with your local authority regulation. If you could get a six-bedroom from one property that would be a money-making machine. The maximum search radius I would go for ½ mile and the price range I am comfortable with lies in the region of £2,500 pcm and the minimum number of bedroom of three. You could perhaps go above the price range of £2,500 pcm subject to profit and return of investment.

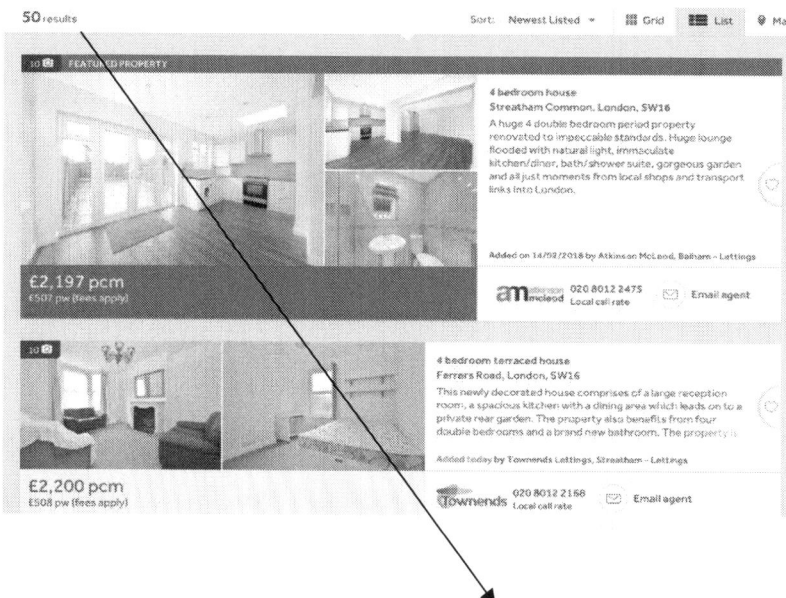

That's the amount of properties being advertised in that criteria.

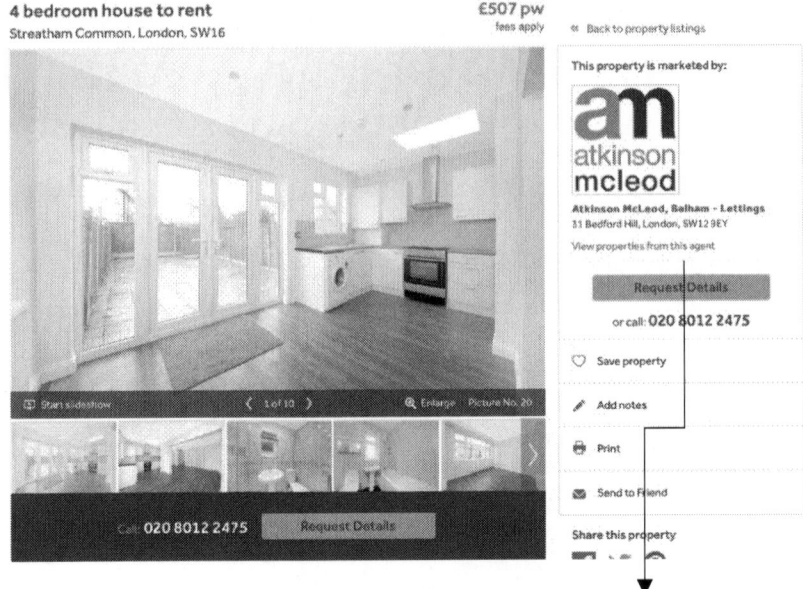

Click on view properties from the agent. This would show all four bedroom houses that this particular agent is advertising and would allow you to book a block viewing.

Another search engine is www.zoopla.co.uk, however, some properties could be advertised on Zoopla and not on Rightmove and vice versa. Therefore, it is important to check both sites. Once on Zoopla, scroll down to the bottom of the page, enter the message in the box and amend to match your requirements. This message would be sent to all clicked agents and they would contact you directly. This approach is very affective as you could get many calls.

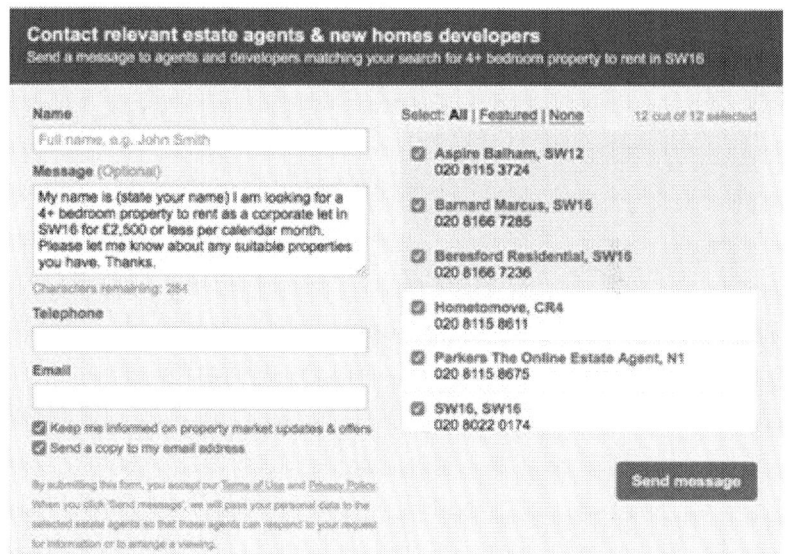

You could also use the websites below to find properties advertised by agents:

www.home.co.uk

www.zoopla.co.uk

www.primelocation.com

www.sequencehome.co.uk

www.rightmove.co.uk

If you prefer going directly to the landlord, below are a few sites where landlords privately advertised their properties:

www.visum.co.uk

www.openrent.co.uk

www.upad.co.uk

www.theonlinelettingagents.co.uk

www.easyproperty.com

www.purplebricks.co.uk

www.gumtree.com

Direct Mail

Another method of getting direct to landlords is via sending them letters about your service. You could obtain addresses through Rightmove or Zoopla. Note that some properties which are advertised would have an Energy Performance Certificate (EPC) attached to it. Another way is through Google Maps. The way I get addresses without going through Google Maps or searching online is to have my partner or friend call the agent and arranged a viewing on the property I wanted to see. Once the agent sends a confirmation text or email with the address, my friend passes it onto me and get them to call the agent to cancel the viewing. Once you have the property's address, you could then go to the Land Registry and get the details of the owner. This gives you the landlord's name and address, who you could then send a letter expressing your interest. In London, this marketing strategy did not really work for me as I sent out a myriad of letters and only got a few replies; none of them securing a deal or showing any level of interest. Associates who operate in London had similar results with zero success on direct mail marketing. However, fast forward to 2019 more landlords in London are being receptive with the letter campaign as I've witnessed great results from my mentees that operate in London. Direct mail marketing works really well if conducted adequately.

HMO List

You could contact your local council under the freedom of information act to obtain an HMO list in the area. This allows you to gain information about properties that already has an HMO license. When contacting the council and requesting the HMO list, you could use the template found at www.napabafikele.com. Some councils have their own HMO list online, so do not forget to browse online too.

Chapter 7 – Analysing Deals

Analysing Deals

Step 5

Step five is analysing deals. Once you find the property and believe the numbers work, before booking a viewing you may want to analyse the deal first. If you book a viewing before analysing and when you get there you find that the numbers do not work, it is a waste of your time, the agent's or landlords'. Therefore, ensure the figures stacked up before making a viewing.

Different trainers will tell you what figures to consider as acceptable profit, depending on where you are in the country. My mentor taught me that in London, select properties that bring a minimum of £800 profit and outside London, £600. However, if it is a deal, I am taking without a JV partner, I would accept a profit of £500 - £600 subject to return on investment. However, if I was doing it with a JV partner, it would have to be a minimum of £800, so that it gives us

£400 each on a 50% split. Note that when securing a deal, you have two costs to keep in mind:

One-off cost: you pay once and that's it:

Deposit

Agent/Reference Fees (if you were doing direct to landlord you could exclude this)

Furnishing cost

Decoration cost

Labour (if you employed someone)

Photographer cost

Monthly cost

Rent

Gas/Electricity

Water

Broadband

Council tax

Cleaner

Let me give you one of my live examples on how I analysed the deal, working out a return on the investment:

Deposit:	*£2,100*
First month rent:	*£2,100*
Agent fee:	*(None as it was direct to landlord)*
Furnishing cost:	*£1,500*
Decoration:	*£250*
Photographer:	*£40*
Total:	**£5,990**

To secure this deal it required £5,990.

The monthly expenses:

Rent:	*£2,100*
Gas / Electricity:	*£173*
Water:	*£30*
Broadband:	*£38*
Council tax:	*£207*
Cleaner:	*£52*
Total:	**£2,562**

The monthly income from each room:

Room 1:	*£750*
Room 2:	*£700*
Room 3:	*£500*
Room 4:	*£620*
Room 5:	*£500*
Room 6:	*£450*
Total:	**£3,520**

To work out your profit, do your Total Room Income, which is £3,520 minus your Total Monthly Expenditure, £2,562 which gives a Net Profit of £958.

To work out your Return on Investment, take the Total Set Up Cost, £5,990; divide by the Net Profit, £958 equaling 6.2 months. Therefore, you know it would take up to 6 months to make your money back from your investment. I would advise that you leave a percentage of the profit for contingency or any unexpected cost that could occur during the business. A common error I made that could have cost me a fortune when I started, was that I wanted to know the weekly and monthly rent for a room. Mistakenly, I had worked out the weekly rental and divided the monthly rental amount by 4 and worked out the monthly rental by multiplying the weekly amount by 4. Now, whenever I speak to people starting up, I am glad to say I was not the only one making this mistake. However, the correct way to work out the weekly and monthly rental amount is as follows:

Monthly: weekly amount x 52/12

E.g.: £150 x 52/12 = £650

Weekly: monthly amount /52x12

E.g.: £650 / 52x12 = £150

Step 6
Putting in an Offer

After viewing the property, you may want to put in an offer in 24 hours. Templates are available at www.napabafikele.com:

Once the offer is accepted, you would go through the references if it is via an agent. In my experience, I went directly to the landlord and they have yet to ask for any references. During the reference process it is the agent's responsibility to identify whether your company can afford the rent and if it is a new company. As discussed earlier, a guarantor would be needed, and they would need to earn 36 times the rental amount and in most occasions be a home owner.

Case Study 7

This property was one of my self-funded deals. I had already built a team around me, so I knew what I was doing. I sourced the deal directly from the landlord, a three-bedroom property with two separate reception rooms.

I first converted the two-reception rooms into double bedrooms. The rent was £1850 and since it was being paid directly to the landlord, I paid a deposit of £1850, the actual rental amount. There were no other fees to be paid.

If you follow me on my social media platform you will see that I really love travelling. When I secured this property I was in Paris, I found the deal online and got my employee to view the property and send me pictures and videos. Since he was working with me for a while, he knew how to do due diligence. He sent me a proposal of how much we could get for each room, since we had properties in that area already, it was very facile to workout figures.

I made the offer to the landlord and it was accepted. I made the payment electronically and arranged for my manager to collect keys. I already had a handy man to purchase furniture and assemble them. That was completed within 24 hours. Another member of the team went to dress the property and finally the photographer went to take professional pictures. The property was fully occupied within a week and the net cash flow was £780.

This is the importance of building your team. There is an old African proverb that says, if you want to go fast go alone but if you want to go far go together. Start building your team as soon you start your property journey. Select people for your team based on certain stringent criteria to ensure the success of your business. The temptation may arise to employ family member and friends. This is okay but remember the relationship will change, so make sure you are protected using formal contracts. Your team should be highly skilled, efficient, flexible and reasonably priced.

Your team will help you to secure deals even when you are not physically present, most importantly manage it.

Napa Bafikele

Chapter 8 – Property Staging

Staging the property

Securing the deal is not a guarantee of success. Your work is not done until you have paying tenants in your property.

Step 7

This step involves property staging. Staging the property is the fun part especially if you are a creative person. The idea is to set up and make the property appealing and inviting, this is to make prospective clients feel at home when they come to view. As the competition for rooms increase, it is important to ensure your property stands out. Most people achieve this by using funky colours and items so that the property remains in the prospects mind. Ikea is the best place to purchase furniture. B&M is another good store for decorations and artistic items. Purchase items that can be reused and are strong enough to be regularly transported from one property to the next without damages. Use complementary colours and subtle tones that can be aesthetically pleasing to a wide market. Try to avoid anything with political slogans, controversial symbols or items with questionable history which may alienate some tenants.

Below is one of my Rent-to-Rent property's which I had set up to stand out and attract the audience I wanted.

Bathroom

- Bright colour matts
- Toilet brush
- Mirror (always ensure there is a mirror in the bathroom)

Kitchen

Microwave

- Utensils
- Kettle
- Toaster
- Art on the wall
- Fire extinguisher (check with local council policy)

If the kitchen is large enough, you could also use it as a communal area. If you were putting a TV in, I would advise that you mount it on the wall as this prevents it from being stolen or tenants moving it around.

Room

- Bed and Mattress
- Study table
- Lamp
- Art on wall
- Wardrobe

If you have a small room, put a large mirror on one wall to create the illusion of space.

Step 8:

Finding tenants

Finding the right tenants is key to your success. To find tenants you could advertise your room on many different websites: The property market continues to boom because of the increased demand and limited supply of housing which makes this area of business the target of many websites that claim to offer solutions but do not add any value. Be careful and always do your due diligence. It may seem cheaper and quicker to do things yourself but always seek out someone who has done it before. Saving a penny early might cost you pounds later. Some websites that I have used in the past to locate potential tenants are:

www.spareroom.co.uk

www.roomgo.co.uk

www.gumtree.com

www.facebook.com

www.openrent.co.uk

Local lettings agents (fees and cost do apply)

www.airbnb.com

Large company firm

Relocation agencies

Recruitment agencies

Local shop windows

During a void (when a room is unoccupied) period you could advertise your property on www.AirBnB.com since people who book short-term tend to end up becoming long-term tenants after a while. I still have a few who have been with me for more than a year after coming from Airbnb. However, using Airbnb during a void period could upset your existing long-term tenants since they may feel unsafe with the constant change in tenants. So, if you were going to use Airbnb to cover your voids, ensure you communicate that effectively across to your long-term tenants.

References:

Once a prospect likes the room and wants to secure it, you should take a holding fee from them and do references to ensure the rent was affordable. You could either use www.homelet.co.uk or NLA to conduct the referencing.

See also:

www.homelet.co.uk

https://www.nlatenantcheck.org.uk

Check in

Once you secured a tenant there are documentation that are legally required and to ensure you are protected from a financial and legal perspective. It is advisable that these documents are completed and signed as early as possible and preferably before a tenant moves into the property. Remember this is business, you have liabilities and certain responsibilities and you must adhere to all of the legal requirements as set out in the law. Do not try to cut corners or act in haste. Get your documents completed and signed.

Once you have secured all the required paperwork, ensure these are filed away. It is a good idea to keep these for a few years before disposing of them. All the required documents and samples can be found at www.napabafikele.com Give them when checking them in.

Case Study 8

One of my mentors told me never to worry about money. If the deal is good, money will show up. I am a living testimony of that. In most of my deals, I used other people's money.

Ornella Jacobs did my 1-2-1 Rent-to-Rent training, then upgraded to my mentoring programme shortly after. She holds the undisputed record of obtaining the quickest deal from my mentoring group. Within 7 days after she completed the training, she sourced a Rent-to-Rent deal directly from a landlord via Gumtree.

Even though I know my programme is worth its value and has a proven track record, I was still amazed. It is important to mention that the deal did not come to find her, she invested a lot of hard work and effort to obtain a deal within 7 days of the mentoring program. She has a strong work ethic and has the right attitude. I always advise my mentees to follow the system I give to them and with hard work, consistency and dedication, success is inevitable.

When Ornella first viewed the property, she called me bursting with excitement, and describing the deal. The property was newly refurbished with six large bedrooms including one ensuite and it already had an HMO license for 6 people. When I asked her about the figures, it was clear she had done her due diligence. The property had the potential to create a healthy profit margin.

One issue Ornella had was the lack of money to finance the deal as she had recently purchased a house. She needed an investor. After my own due diligence, I took the deal and offered to be her joint venture partner by financing the deal and splitting the profit.

We structured the deal in a smart way where our entry cost was lower than expected by offsetting some of the initial costs using various methods. A total investment of £3145 secured the deal. The landlord was very nice and accommodating as he understood the value, we were offering him. The profit for this current deal is £913 meaning that I make my initial investment back within three months and get paid monthly after for the three years' lifetime of the deal. For Ornella, she obtained a deal where she did not put any of her money and she is making a massive profit from it.

Case Study 9

This property is a Rent-to-Rent deal sourced by my mentees Duquarn and Kingsley. They have been a part of my mentoring group since 2016. The deal was sourced through an agent their knew before. Their already had an history of working with the agent, having sourced several deals through them.

Duquarn and Kingsley just released a four-bedroom flat from their portfolio to restructure the business and adapt to the current climate. Their want to remain in the Rent-to-Rent market but shift their focus to the higher end of the market via targeting higher cashflow properties.

Their saw a deal online and decided to call the agent straight away as it met their new criteria. The property was located five minutes away from Norbury Rail station and consisted of three floors with five potential bedrooms, two communal kitchens, two bathrooms and one en-suite. The property was originally advertised for £1900 and at first the landlord objected to the property being rented as a multi-let.

However, a lack of interest from the open market and weeks of negotiating convinced him to change his mind. Duquarn and Kingsley secured a deal on the property for just £1700 for 3 years. There are currently going through with an application with the council for the property to be HMO licensed. Once this is finalised the total income with all rooms being rented will amount to £3180. After utilities (£400) and rent (£1700) had been paid it will allow them to net a stunning figure of £1080.

Chapter 9 – Hiring a Property Manager

Most entrepreneurs when they are starting out on their journey will remain in their full-time employment just for the added security it offers, then slowly transition into a full-time business owner. This is perfectly manageable with one or the maximum two properties although you may still need some flexibility in your full-time day job. Working for an organisation that require you to be physically present and visible 9-5pm may impact on your business unless you have reliable people in your life.

You should always prepare for possible emergency scenarios that require you to attend a property quickly to offer some resolutions or solutions.

Ideally once you get to 4 or 5 properties you may want to consider hiring a property manager to look after your portfolio, freeing up your time. However, I would say that within the first few deals, you managed them by yourself so that you could gain the experience on how it works. The knowledge and experience you acquire could then be passed onto your potential property manager. However, hiring a property manager would be an additional cost to your business, therefore, ensure you have a strong enough cashflow. I hired one such manager. This tenant was in one of my properties, he was very good and keen on the business. He was working in retail and got fed up with his job, so he was looking for a different challenge. He asked if I was hiring for a position in my company and I gladly started teaching him the necessary skills to secure a property manager's position. His responsibilities were:

- Tenant screening
- Viewings
- Deal with issues
- Administration

I paid him £100 per property which was deducted from the property profit and whenever he secures a tenant, I paid him £50 commission. If the property was under 80% occupied, there was a different payment structure.

If you are considering hiring a manager further down the line on your property journey, it is vital to start documenting as you go along, creating a booklet that you could pass onto the relevant person. In my Rent-to-Rent Manual I include a section with all the relevant job descriptions and expectations that the person must sign as a contract to ensure there are no mistakes when it comes to compensation for the work done. I have documented how I screen tenants, conduct viewings, advertise and source tenants. I also have a list of the contractors in the area and all the manager needs to do is go to the list and contact the relevant contractor should he need one. The booklet also has login details for all online portals I use, and we use www.dropbox.com to store our files which is easy to update online.

Chapter 10 – Types of Contracts

Contract Types

In this chapter I address the different types of agreements you could use, however, for you to be certain I recommend consulting a solicitor or a specialist in this area. If you are still unsure on what to do, get in touch.

Agreements between Property Owners and the Rent-to-Renter

Depending on how the property is encumbered, the type of property will determine the type of agreement you should use. It will also have implications for any taxation.

Listed below are the following agreements which are about the arrangements between the property owner and your rent to rent company.

Do Not Use an Assured Shorthold Tenancy:

Some agents only want to use an Assured Shorthold Tenancy (AST). The AST is never the right agreement since it is only suitable for individuals as defined in Section 1) Clause 1) Sub-clause A-C of the Housing Act 1988. _You cannot use this agreement in any circumstances_ and if they insist, they misunderstand the business you are in.

Management Agreement:

This agreement is between your company and the landlord. It is also the type of agreement letting agents use with the landlord on their portfolio.

Mortgage companies are used to management agreements, therefore, it is a suitable form of agreement to use when the landlord has a mortgage on the property. You must be aware that the income you are receiving is a mixture of Rental and Management Fees and the management fees element is a taxable supply, so when you have a business with sufficient management fees you may need to register for VAT. At that stage you will have a very big business and a profitable one too. Please _seek accountancy advice on this as domestic rental_ *income is VAT exempt where management fees are not.*

Company Let Agreement:

This agreement is used where a corporate entity wishes to rent the entire property from a landlord. The company can rent the entire property with the sole purpose of renting it to their employees. You cannot use the Housing Act laws to enforce this tenancy - only common law. This means that to terminate you issue a Notice to Quit rather than Section 8 or 21 Notices to obtain possession. The deposit also does not need to be secured in an approved Tenancy Deposit Scheme, though it is advised that any deposit is retained in an appropriate Client's Account with any agent, landlord or property manager and that they have suitable Client Money protection procedures and insurances in place.

In its purest form it is not the most appropriate for rent-to-rent since we would not be putting our own employees in the property. A suitably drafted different and similar agreement can be used.

Common Law Tenancy/Non Housing Act Tenancy:

In using this type of tenancy - the most popular with letting agents - you must ensure that you structure your agreements correctly. The agreement with the occupants must always expire before the agreement with the Property Owner. If the agreement with the occupants is equal to or greater than the agreement with the Property Owner, then this will usually result in the assignment of your agreement to the occupants and this is not what the parties intend.

In this agreement you must ensure that any ability to create tenancies for your occupants is permitted, that subletting is permitted and that any mortgages on the property permit the property to be used as a House in Multiple Occupation (HMO). In addition, ensuring that the owner has the relevant consents in place and can let on a Non Housing Act Tenancy from his mortgage company and insurance providers.

Commercial Lease:

Sometimes called a Landlord and Tenant Act 1954 Lease; this agreement is suitable for properties where the owner has no mortgage and is totally unencumbered. As there are little restrictions on the owner, have this lease drawn up professionally and ensure the insurance policies operate for the use. This is the best option, when done and the matters about security of tenure are handled correctly and will work well for you. Also, remember that 63% of UK properties are unencumbered, so there is a lot of opportunity here.

Agreements between the Rent-to-Renter and the Tenants

There are two types of agreements that can be used depending on the situation for the tenant:

1) It is their only or principal home; then you use an Assured Shorthold Tenancy Agreement;

2) If they are staying temporarily and have a principle or only home elsewhere, or they are staying for a holiday, then you use a License Agreement.

Assured Shorthold Tenancy Agreement (AST):

This is a statutory tenancy and you must follow procedures properly and within the confines of the Housing Act 1988. So, deposits must be protected in an approved Tenancy Deposit Protection Schemes. Possession procedures must adhere to the Housing Acts, the popular Section 8 for rent arrears and other breaches and the Section 21 Notice for time expired claims.

There are many dependencies on providing prescribed information at the commencement of the tenancy and ongoing compliance to be able to serve any possession notice during a tenancy. See advice on issuing a tenancy from qualified persons.

License Agreement:

This agreement is mainly used when the occupier is staying short-term - under 3 months in most cases - and has a principle home elsewhere that they can return to at any time. Its use must be appropriate since it is known that some operators use this agreement extensively and incorrectly It will be viewed and considered as an AST by the courts if it is apparent the occupant is living in the property as his principle residence.

Using the agreement, expecting to give occupants shorter notice periods may work in the opposite direction too and the occupant can give equally short notice.

Agreements in General

Please ensure you get the agreements right, get the right properties, the right people and the right agreements and you will have great contractual foundations for a strong business.

Case Study 10

In under 3 months, I have been mentoring Daniel and he has already secured his first deal. The property was sourced via an agent and the landlord applied for the HMO license which was granted. The landlord promised to paint the property; however, it was not done to the standards required and the agency offered Daniel to take complimentary photographs as well as advertise at their expense.

Monthly Cost:	£	Income:	£
Rent:	2,200	Room 1:	900
Council tax:	101	Room 2:	850
Water:	30	Room 3:	850
Broadband:	28	Room 4:	800
Gas/Electricity:	170		
Cleaner:	40		
Total:	**2,569**	**Total:**	**3,400**
Profit:			**831**

Testimonials

Daniel Dodgson

I first met Napa in October 2018. After curiously joining a Facebook group specially for Rent-to-Rent HMO's, I got speaking with him. He offered to meet with me so that he could answer my questions of which there were hundreds. Two months later, after signing Napa as my mentor, I managed to secure my first Rent-to-Rent HMO. He has been at the end of a call, text or email every single day, answered everything I asked in detail, including attending viewings with me. Most importantly, he has been encouraging and making sure I have not allowed myself to slip back into my comfort zone, maintaining the work necessary to grind out the results.

Norris Ngwamah

In every business you wished to venture into, there is always some sort of skeptical thoughts that jumped out at you, either causing you to delay or completely stop. It is a bit like some sort of cage fight. I wrestled with the idea of starting a Rent-to-Rent business after hearing the success stories and being unable to see the other side of the coin for myself. It was not until Napa, my friend, who had decided to take the first step into Rent-to-Rent, and I saw how hard he worked plus the fruits it gave him that I decided to start my business. I guess I needed someone close to me to tell me that it was possible. I then decided to get off my backside and do something. With Napa's help and guidance, I have managed to secure two properties that brought me and my business partner net profits of £1,000 for each property. I guess what I was afraid of is not so much to step onto the Rent-to-Rent ladder but that I just needed someone to guide me through it. This made all the difference. Someone you could relate to, who encouraged you as well as kept it real.

Guy Nzanza

Working with Napa must be one of the best experiences I have gone through. His natural confidence influences you to do better and try harder in every aspect of life. Learning the Rent-to-Rent business was not as easy as I had thought, but by being patient and understanding, I was able to learn at my own pace. Napa also gave me the best advice which in turn raised my own confidence. From the start we set short- and long-term goals, going through them regularly to make sure I was on track with everything I wanted to do. This allowed me to remain focused on the things I needed to prioritise, and organise my time efficiently in order to get everything done. Every week he called to catch up with what I had done during the week, and this was where we set appointments to discuss matters. Whenever I came across anything I had not understood, I gave him a call and discussed it further. if he was not free, he would call at his earliest convenience. The fact that he was flexible and adapted to any given situation made me appreciate his teaching even much more. ☐☐This was my testimonial for you...Thank you again Napa for offering me your mentoring aide.

Kingsley Nkwocha

If it was not for Napa, we would not be in property at all. We first met him in early 2016, working as estate agents for one of the high street brands. He called up a few times regarding something called 'corporate lets' and the agency we worked for always told us to automatically reject calls and people of this nature but in this case, we wanted to know a little bit more about what he was doing. We exchanged numbers and met shortly after where he totally blew our minds with his knowledge, confidence and professionalism especially since we all were the same age! He told us all about Rent-to-Rent and how we could get started. We could not wait to put what he had taught us into practice. When we left our day jobs, he mentored and guided us from property and tenant issues to legislative updates. We leveraged his experience to avoid pitfalls and capitalised on opportunities without any fear of failure. In times of hardship within the business, he always lent an ear to listen to as well as gave words of wisdom and encouragement.

Napa was extremely motivational and a total inspiration to us and we owe our property career hugely to him for giving us the template and setting such high standards for us. To date, we currently managed seven properties and have a net profit of about £3,800pcm. In 2019, we were looking to venture into buying property across the UK and hopefully even joint venture with Napa. Thank you, Napa, for giving us the confidence to do this, you've changed our lives.

Trisha Nzau

In such a small space of time Napa has added so much value to my journey. Before I met him, I had low confidence and limited knowledge of R2R. I went to several training days and crash courses but did not get enough out of them. I now have a lot more confidence and a better understanding on how the business works. I was comfortable going as far as dealing with agents over the phone since I avoided face-to-face contact and was worried about rejection. There were times I wanted to give up and Napa reassured me that throughout the journey, I was more likely to get more no's than yes's, but not giving up would get me that yes. He taught me that there were no lines or scripts when talking to agents but to give them all the answers they needed and if I did not know, simply say I could find out. Napa held me accountable for every step of my journey to date.

Napa's extensive experience helped me pick my goldmine area since he knows the growth of London well and which areas would work best. He also emphasised how to be compliant with laws and regulations and contact the local council whenever I needed confirmation on the best way to do something. Meeting Napa was by far the highlight of my journey as he put a lot of things into perspective and helped me overcome the barriers that restricted me from progressing. He genuinely wants everyone to succeed.☐Great guy, I could not thank him more.☐

Glossary of Rent-to-Rent Terms

Abbreviation	Term	Notes
BTL	Buy-to-Let	A property purchased with a sole purpose to rent out
PCM	Per Calendar Month	An amount that is produced, sold or spent each month
HMO	House in Multiple Occupation	A residential property where residents have private rooms but share common areas
JV	Joint Venture	When two parties agree to partner on a project for an agreed, mutual gain or profit
R2R	Rent-to-Rent	A property as a single let and re-let as a multi let
EPC	Energy Performance Certificate	A summary rating of energy efficiency of a property
AST	Assured Short hold Tenancy	A tenancy agreement between landlord/agency and a tenant.

My Final Word

I would like to thank you for taking your time to read and finish this book, I really hope it has given so much value and confidence to you, to begin your own Rent-to-Rent journey. Encouraged by a realistic mindset and prepared mentality for obstacles that could arise. If you would like to contact me on how I could help you start your Rent-to-Rent journey, you may find me on the following platforms:

Facebook: Napa G Bafikele

Instagram: napa_bafikele

LinkedIn: Napa Bafikele

If you would like me to mentor you, please visit my website to see packages available:

Website: www.napabafikele.com

Why not join our Facebook group - The Rent2Rent Entrepreneur with Napa Bafikele

https://www.facebook.com/groups/329191747913769/

Sources:

http://worldpopulationreview.com/countries/united-kingdom-population/

https://www.readersdigest.co.uk/money/property/how-to-understand-the-housing-crisis

https://www.ons.gov.uk/peoplepopulationandcommuni ty/populationandmigration/populationestimates/article s/overviewoftheukpopulation/july2017

NOTES:

47277349R00101

Printed in Poland
by Amazon Fulfillment
Poland Sp. z o.o., Wrocław